BEYOND OUR DEGREES *of* SEPARATION

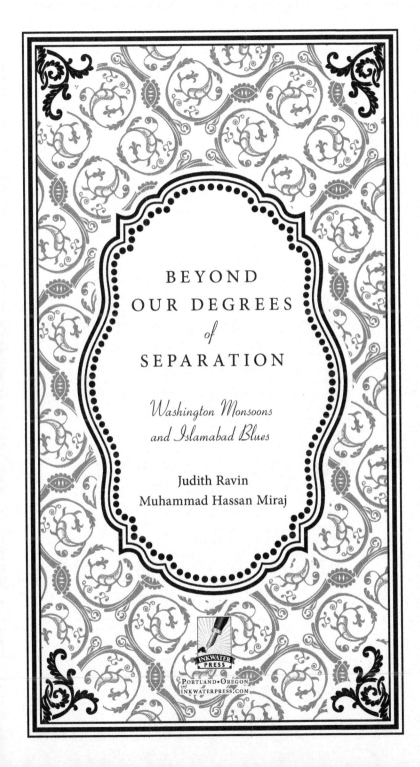

BEYOND OUR DEGREES

of

SEPARATION

*Washington Monsoons
and Islamabad Blues*

Judith Ravin
Muhammad Hassan Miraj

INKWATER
PRESS

PORTLAND•OREGON
INKWATERPRESS.COM

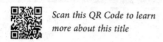

*Scan this QR Code to learn
more about this title*

Mi'rāj, Muḥammad Ḥasan, author.
    Beyond our degrees of separation / by Muhammad Hassan
Miraj & Judith Ravin.
    pages cm
    LCCN 2017900838
    ISBN 978-1-62901-454-8 (pbk.)
    ISBN 978-1-62901-455-5 (Kindle ebk.)
    ISBN 978-1-62901-456-2 (ePub ebk.)

    1. Ravin, Judith, 1958---Travel--Pakistan.
    2. Diplomats--United States--Biography. 3. Diplomats--
    Pakistan--Biography. 4. Pakistan--Description and
    travel. 5. Mi'rāj, Muḥammad Ḥasan--Travel--United
    States. 6. Pakistan. Army--Biography. 7. United States
    --Description and travel. 8. Pakistan--Foreign
    relations--United States. 9. United States--Foreign
    relations--Pakistan. 10. Autobiographies.   I. Ravin,
    Judith, 1958- author. II. Title.

    DS377.M49 2017   915.49104'532
                              QBI17-900041

Publisher: Inkwater Press | www.inkwaterpress.com

Paperback   ISBN-13 978-1-62901-454-8 | ISBN-10 1-62901-454-0
Kindle   ISBN-13 978-1-62901-455-5 | ISBN-10 1-62901-455-9
ePub   ISBN-13 978-1-62901-456-2 | ISBN-10 1-62901-456-7

Printed in the U.S.A.

1 3 5 7 9 10 8 6 4 2

DEDICATION

For my sister, who prodded me to share my periplus.

JUDITH RAVIN

For Ammi and her ever-present interest in my stories
And through stories, an opening, for Abbu.

MUHAMMAD HASSAN MIRAJ

"We are nothing but the stories we tell and the stories we live."

–Muhammad Hassan Miraj

TABLE OF CONTENTS

BEYOND OUR DEGREES

OF SEPARATION

INTRODUCTION

MY JOURNEY LED ME TO HIS LAND, AND HIS journey led him to mine. Paths that had no reason to cross converged. As our stories unraveled and connectors formed, a deliberate merge in memory became a way to portray the unexpected commonality between an American woman in Pakistan and a Pakistani man yearning for his homeland – mirror images of transposed experiences.

Within the stirrings of memory, the encounter between an American diplomat on assignment to Pakistan and a U.S.-trained member of the Pakistani military occurred around the periphery of a small courtyard, where a crowd gathered mid-morning on a sun-drenched lawn. Early spring in Pakistan's capital city was finally taking hold.

The first conversation was fluid – too fluid, in fact, for two strangers who had just met with seemingly nothing in common beyond joint advocacy for the event at hand, a celebration of the art of handwritten letters in contributing to public and private history. From letter-writing to screenplays, to poetry and prose, the off-hand discussion of that first encounter led to exchanges on other topics over the months, ultimately transforming the thread of a long-gone conversation into the yarn of potential creation. Fact and fiction were in the offing, though to what extent was unclear. The two stories could have continued on a parallel course. Dissimilar worlds need not touch. But the contours of an emerging warp were so unavoidably apparent, the question soon became how, not whether, to join the two narratives. *Beyond Our Degrees of Separation* is the exploration of that weft moving transversely through the fabric of our lives. Its weave is proof that travel and fate obey their own logic.

YESTERDAY AND TOMORROW

WITH ACCUMULATING JETLAG PLUS A MESH OF sunsets missed and sunrises gained, the blend of yesterday takes me through the first couple of days following my arrival in Islamabad. Suffice it to say that in Urdu, the national language of Pakistan, the word employed to mean "yesterday" is identical to the word used to indicate "tomorrow." The fact embodies symbolism beyond coincidence.

The car from the airport road breezed through several security checkpoints with little need for the electronic assistance of traffic lights, most of which were not working anyway at two o'clock in the morning. Passing vehicles in either direction were limited. A fresh rain had just coated the city, leaving generous puddles where the surface was broken up into concave pockets. In the slower, left-hand lane, a lone truck with a baroque front-piece and brightly painted sideboards belied its utilitarian cargo of fuel. Sidelights illuminated the hammered-metal arc over the cab, furthering the disproportionate decoration of the short front-piece relative to its heavy rear load. Like a centerpiece on the move, art and cargo made their way through the wee hours.

According to an article that came out twenty-four hours later, that same night shortly after midnight a police raid of a village home on the outskirts of Islamabad uncovered a parked car in the driveway with 125 kilograms of explosives strapped inside the two doors on the driver's side. The authorities' inspection determined the explosives would have been activated via remote control, though the intended target had not yet been established.

Ignorant of the foiled potential incident in the lead-up hours to my arrival and content to be out of the air and on the ground, I reached my new home in darkness. Despite the hour, I drew the curtains for a look through a top-floor window. In silhouette the surrounding ridgetops of the Margalla Hills filled the frame with the wonderment of a fresh reference point. Too much newness made the idea of sleep impossible, once again. Nearing four thirty in the morning the first of five calls to prayer would ring out from minarets in the city. Eventually, the sun would rise, bringing to a close my yesterday, issuing in tomorrow.

HAMLETS OF
THE NORTH

O N THE ROAD THAT CONNECTED SKARDU, Pakistan, with Kargil, India (pre-1947 Partition), there is a turn that runs through Shigar. The road is less travelled but the turn is not. Kargil shot to fame after the 1999 conflict in Kashmir, though the road had met a dead end half a century earlier. The last address on this turn is K-2. Between the turn and Shigar hangs a wooden bridge that allows one vehicle to pass at a time. Strangely though, no one honks the horn, and no one revs the engine. Take a turn, and one can see sand dunes running parallel to a river, with mountains standing along one side as witness. A desert, a river, and a mountain range — topographical features that made half of my seventh-grade geography book – can be seen in one visual.

It is quite difficult to tell the difference between sunrise and sunset in Shigar, a small village that claims to be a town because of the presence of a few district offices. The handiest marker is the sound of watermills, powered by springs, which are nearly silent at sunrise but very loud at the sunset.

I was twice reminded of USA in this almost non-global corner of Pakistan. The first reminder was through Tahereh. I met her on the lawn of Fong-Khar, a palace-cum-fort of the former local ruler that also served as a tourist resort and hotel. Raja Hassan Ali Amacha, or Raja (as the locals address him) lived next door in a large purpose-built house. (Although the position of *raja* is constitutionally abolished since 1974, locals still use this honorific of the vernacular for "ruler.") Tahereh had come to the hotel to check her email, as this was the only place with internet connectivity. Against the auburn background of the hills, her ash-like hair symbolized the ancient Jogi tradition. Tahereh, a non-resident Pakistani-American with interest in garden design and hiking, had a house in California, though her heart seemed to reside in the mountains of northern Pakistan. A casual look at images of a 60-year-old German couple trekking to Ghondogoro La had captured her imagination, filling the gap between envy toward those mad hatters and donning one herself.

In 2009, as her payback to mountain communities, she offered to consult with Aga Khan Cultural Services Pakistan (AKCSP) to help design a garden at a school they had built in the village of Siankhor, in Shigar. For the next couple of years, there was no summer for her in California. What ended after a two-month consultancy

6

with AKCSP started a six-year volunteer project to raise funds for the garden and to train teachers in the use of that space as a classroom to learn by doing. The school was the first of its kind in the Northern Areas, and the concept is the first of its kind in Pakistan, barring a few similar experiments in Karachi. In the school gardens, flowerbeds are the boxed worksheets for arithmetic, growing vegetables connects to biology, and the stories of potatoes and tomatoes form the basis for grammar lessons. Tahereh now splits her time between California and Shigar. Hers is the story of human spirit and selfless commitment to the betterment of the human race.

The second reminder came from Baltit, a smaller village of Hunza, now known as Karimabad. Baltit reminds one of some magical land of fairy tales. Dreamlike mist surrounds the landscape, and almost everything appears mythical, at first, including the locals. Beg was no exception.

Trained as a mountain guide, it was while negotiating the silent snow dunes that Beg also acquired the skill set that was rather integral to his profession: the art of storytelling. He was a fabulous storyteller and probably the last of those few who still believed that the greatest human experience was the hippie trail of the 1960s and 70s, and John Lennon.

Beg was as straight-forward as his great-great-grandfather, who happened to be the local ruler, the Mir (Chief) of Hunza. At the height of the Great Game, Hunza was where British and Russian agents would often run into each other. Francis Younghusband was a

British military officer who was travelling to these areas on his own accord. Once he reached Hunza, in the year 1889 of his Lord, he was taken to the Mir. It was not just the grandeur of the Mir that struck him but also his nearly delusional self-confidence. So when he asked the Mir what exactly he thought about the size of the British Empire (this was at the time the sun would not set on the Empire), the Mir responded:

"Maybe slightly larger than Hunza, if not the same." Hunza was at that time nothing more than a combination of a few villages with a total population of slightly over one thousand.

Beg had not only travelled to the U.S. but also planned to settle down there. During one of his trekking tours, he had rescued the life of a young woman from Cincinnati, who was deeply grateful to him. She instantly invited Beg to her place. Since it was a routine matter for Beg to have tourists inviting him for trips, he did not take the invitation seriously. Weeks later, he received a more formal invitation to make the journey. Beg hesitantly asked his father, who thought for a day and then granted him permission with a comeback clause. Beg could proceed to the United States only after his marriage. As if travelling off to adventure in the United States was not enough of a thrill, the Cincinnati woman happened to know Neil Armstrong, a man who had impressed Beg. Together, they went to see him and ended up living with him as honored guests for some time.

Despite all the good things in the free world, Beg

changed his mind. One day as he lay down and compared his time in Cincinnati with his life in Hunza, Beg realized that happiness was not what he believed. It was a moment that he shared with Prince Hamlet.

"To be or not to be…"

The enlightened, the wise, or the otherwise Beg returned home to his aging father and young bride who still had his photos neatly kept in single-leaf albums in a walnut chest of drawers.

For all those who travel to Hunza and come across Beg, a tea at his place is a must, served alongside American pancakes, stored in the same walnut chest of drawers.

If I were to describe Beg, I would simply call him the candy store of stories.

PRE-MONSOON EID

THE CLOUDS HANG LOW ON THE HIMALAYAN FOOT-hills as the imam's call to prayer drifts along the landscape keeping pace with the wind. For those withstanding the soaring temperatures of summer, without food or water, the change in rhythm and rigor is welcome.

Under wraps, the thunder rumbles. Distant lightning in flashes presages an onslaught of rain. For hours the deluge feels imminent, yet no drops fall to settle the dust and debris whirling about in futile circles above the ground. The sky at sunset is painted over in strokes of gray and black, moving the dusk to nightfall with little transition.

All eyes are on the crescent moon. If sighted, it heralds the beginning of the feast to follow another year's fasting during the holy month of Ramazan.*

With reduced light and increasing drama skyward, the elements exercise an enhanced effect on the psyche, inducing a state of willful reflection. During the past

---

* *Ramazan*, or *Ramzan*, is the Urdu equivalent of Ramadan.

month humanity has amassed at crossroads across the city, beckoning passersby to consider helping out the less fortunate. Charitable contributions at this time of year are said to multiply the rewards.

Among one-off encounters that throw a disturbing light upon the darkened backdrop is a teenage girl moving on hands and knees through traffic. There is no way to spot her in the darkness unless one happens to be slowing down for a turn. Money or a handout may be sufficient for her but, from the driver's perspective, getting her off the road and back onto the grassy divider is the best form of charity, even if her condition proves to be a malady of the mind and ruse to earn a few meals.

Another long shadow of recollection is cast by an emergency stop at a tire repair hangar set alongside the road. Like a doctor examining a splinter of wood in soft flesh, the young auto-mechanic is quick to locate a nail embedded in the tire. He points out the puncture wound, adding a few drops of water that bubble as air escapes slowly from around the nail. He has seen this an infinite number of times, and it requires little concentration for him to carry out the routine repair. An incoming call on his cell leaves the mobile cocked between shoulder and ear as he patches the hole in the tire. With a single hand he completes the repair, saving the other to gesticulate animatedly while in conversation with his unseen interlocutor.

Unconvinced that the repairman's divided attention has resulted in careful workmanship, I ask if the remedy is definitive. The entire job was done with one hand, while talking on the phone. Our eyes lock. The mechanic need not interrupt his mobile connection for this additional inquiry. He spits on his finger, using the same hand that executed the repair, and applies the fresh spittle to the patched hole where the nail had been. The bubbling water is no more. The work has silenced it.

At the rate of a dollar or less per repair, the matter he is discussing by phone may well be worth more than the utility of relegating to assist a second hand actively engaged in negotiation through gesture.

The pre-Monsoon rains on the eve of Eid finally release their hold on the wetness in the clouds. The foot-hills bordering Islamabad to the north take in the rain. Paved and unpaved roads throughout the city are swept clean of drive-by clientele, crawling, spittle, and all.

FATIMA TO FATIMA

DURING THE LAST PART OF MY FIELD STUDY TOUR, a week-long visit to Washington DC was scheduled for the international students. The travel day of the visit coincided with Eid-ul-Fitr, which similar to Christmas is only a real celebration when one is home. For all its festivity, Eid's truest colors are felt in one's country of origin. Its celebration in the United States, however, made me realize how complex it was to transpose "home" onto the new environment in the Western Hemisphere.

Throughout Eid in the Muslim diaspora, mosques and religious centers are filled with people wearing mostly ill-fitting finery, stitched according to measurements dictated over the phone to distant tailors, or in sizes their users have either grown out of or not yet grown into. While festivity is in the air inside the halls of these structures, a mess awaits commuters outside. Out of sheer jubilation for the occasion, many celebrants park their cars against the better judgment of logic or stall traffic while greeting each other midway.

The day begins with special Eid prayers. In Pakistan, adherence to the timings is a no-nonsense affair since everything revolves around the prayers, but on the American side of the globe it is kept flexible. In most countries throughout the Global North, Eid is not a public holiday. Prayers are therefore held in three shifts – 7:00, 8:00, and 9:00 in the morning – to suit the convenience of devotees.

It was halfway through Eid celebrations, when the other international students and I started our journey to Washington DC. Traversing Oklahoma and Dallas took a while, but thanks to varying time zones, we reached the capital by 1:30 in the afternoon. Our stay was arranged at a hotel that sits next to the office of Rand Corporation and takes its insignia from a version of the lion seen by John of the Book of Revelations. The Potomac River divides DC from Virginia, the state famed for the military Mecca of the world, the Pentagon. Moving elevators, stalls alongside the road, Macy's at the back, and a super mall next door were all the blessings of a free economy.

On day two of our visit, we went to Capitol Hill. Raised by the U.S. Army Corps of Engineers and designed for building seats of government, the structure is a reminder of American influence across the globe. A statue of freedom sits atop its dome, with all that accompanies such ancient symbolism. Inside, the history of settlement is told through a series of paintings. At the most interesting and inspiring of these, the guide made it a point to stop and explain to us students, who mainly came from either Arab countries or those with a damaged democratic track record, that this is George Washington, who resigned his military commission before becoming president. The guide's glance met our wandering eyes looking elsewhere.

We then moved to the Vietnam Veterans Memorial, remembrance for a war that divided the nation. It was designed as a wall that symbolized a scar between the Washington Monument and the Capitol, and contained the names of over 58,000 fallen soldiers. Not far from this memorial was also the site of the most famous speech of Martin Luther King, Jr., "I Have a Dream," a dream that still, probably, has a long way to go.

From one memorial to another, and from one history to another, the tale of magnificence is told to an endless flow of audiences, in a manner that remains etched in their memory. At the Lincoln Memorial, the Roman columns guard an imposing statue of a seated Lincoln, both stressed and relaxed, in part, due to a troubled married life and, in part, due to his satisfaction with the achievement of prosperity in the United States.

We were then taken to the Korean War Veterans Memorial, a very artistic and thematic memorial that had 19 soldiers from varying ethnic backgrounds giving a reflection of another 19, thus symbolizing the 38 months (3 years, 1 month, and 2 days, to be exact) of the war and the 38th Parallel, a geographical reference to the border between North and South Korea prior to the war.

Next was the Thomas Jefferson Memorial, a tribute

to the most inspiring statesman of all the founding fathers. The structure now overlooks the White House. Of all things moving, I liked Jefferson's quote about adjusting the coat worn as a boy to that of a man, stressing the need to alter social values in step with the changes in society.

The last stop on the tour was the Memorial for Franklin Delano Roosevelt (FDR), the only president to have been elected to four terms in office. His advocacy on behalf of one-third of the nation that was "ill-housed, ill-clad, ill-nourished" resulted in many irrigation projects, social security reforms, and infrastructure developments.

The guide stopped suddenly and informed us that an orchard had previously occupied the site, but as FDR wanted to see all of the construction going on around the Capitol and had an obstructed view from the White House, he ordered that the cherry trees gifted by Japan be cut down.

"So there is a history of a strained relationship before Hiroshima," remarked the South Korean military officer.

A day filled with memorials ended in a rather memorable way. It was a scheduled dinner where the defense attachés would walk in and talk to their country's officers from the course. The chief guest was a three-star general with a memory full of stories, though just the military ones. On my way to a second helping, I spotted a South Asian face. Before I was stung by the wave of indecisiveness that hits every South Asian when he spots another, the gentleman forwarded his hand and greeted me, *"Assalam o alaikum."*

From a day of amazing history and awe-inspiring stress, nothing sounded more pleasant. What followed was even more promising. The man was a Bangladeshi-American who was serving as an officer in the U.S. Navy as well as an imam within the institution. The more I talked to him, the more I realized how religion could actually bring human beings together rather than divide them.

We exchanged contact details and, before the good-bye, his daughter walked up to me and asked how many kids I had. A rather mature question, but you could expect anything from children these days, so I replied that I had one, a daughter.

"You can tell her that Fatima sends her love," was her response.

I was startled. From a place far away from home, one Fatima was sending love to another Fatima. At one point in time in the blood-soaked history of our two countries, both would have even shared the same nationality.

A sentence from my all-time favorite movie echoed in my mind. "All I ever wanted was a world without maps."

FOUR BLIND
BROTHERS

POETRY SPRINGS FROM THE SPIRITUAL HEART OF Pakistan. Tender and vulnerable like a first love, the pining for poetry is among its citizens' lasting pleasures. Over the centuries, national poet masters – through song or verse – have continued to inspire new generations in the tradition of aesthetic bravado.

As a prelude to an evening of instrumental music and to warm up the audience, the poet stood before the crowd, seated cross-legged on pillows and carpet, and spoke of four brothers of the Muslim faith – an Arab, a Turk, a Pakistani, and an American – who were over-heard arguing about what to do with the arrival in their midst of a handsome sum in silver coins.

After some time for contemplation, each was to state what he would do with the modest fortune, should it come his way, and his way only. Their collective thought was that if the coins were to be divided up into four equal parts, no one would be able to realize his life's dreams. So, attempting to convince the others that he possessed sole justification for putting the entire sum toward the glory of his project, each revealed the business plan he had in mind.

"Ainab," said the Arab. It was a project of unquestionable value.

"Üzüm," countered the Turk, firm in the belief that his initiative was built on solid business principles.

"Angoor," was all the Pakistani had to say, so purposeful was his mission and so simple was his trajectory toward project completion.

"Grapes," said the American.

As each expounded on the reason for why the entirety of the bonanza should come his way, a passerby happened upon the gathering and listened in. He considered the discussion futile and asked the group to hand over to him the full battery of metal coins. He claimed to have a solution that would settle the matter once and for all. The offer of a third party, neutral to their conflicting interests, put them at ease. A state of regained trust in one another settled over the four. Since they had made little progress in arguing among themselves anyway, the group agreed to the proposition of the fifth gentleman, outside their circle, and they gave him the collection of silver coins. All held dear to the hope that new wealth born of new-found wealth was close at hand.

The bystander took the money, went to the market, and came back with grapes, for he alone had noted that all four project exponents had utilized the same word in the vernacular of the respective speakers.

The poet leaned in toward his by-now transfixed listeners. "If we could only step back and try to work together more often, putting aside our seeming differences, we might find that we are actually all wishing for the same thing."

WE ALL SERVE
KNOWLEDGE

A STREAM THAT RUNS ALONG A DENSELY WOODED forest on one side creates movement along the barely inhabited bank, sending rushes of cool water and a slow breeze upward into the only structure visible for kilometers around. Out of the unassuming climb in the road, an ornate building rises to the right of the hilly incline before the road turns.

Inside, young boys rock back and forth gently over pages of the Quran that contain a day's lesson in verses. Day after day, in an uneven hum, they plow through the texts, keeping the room abuzz in a rhythm of shared concentration.

In a town with limited schooling options and no hospital, this college of religious learning bridges time and circumstance. Over the years, the ranks have thickened. Some boys come to fulfill the wishes of parents eager to have a family member poised to advocate on their behalf through prayer and devotion. Others are swept up into the system, the result of parental abandonment or loss. Absent any other gesture of solidarity, this one is at least real.

To ease society's burden, the man behind the madrassa – himself a product of years of religious study – opens the opportunity of Islamic learning to the youth that land on his doorstep. In return, they receive a constant regiment of religious teaching, simple clothing, food, and a place to rest their heads when a long day's reading and reciting comes to a close.

For the residents living among the hillside's beauty, this private act of charity fills a gap. Local authorities might have stepped in at any point but did not, except once to close a hospital the community had built. Perhaps there was resentment toward the competition, or doubts about adherence to the health code. Bureaucratic bickering aside, the town is without sufficient grade school facilities in the immediate vicinity.

So here the boys do what the girls cannot. They serve the greater cause of knowledge. Their surroundings speak of a tradition that is a thousand years old, as the young scholars take up where others left off. The new students' beginnings are the older students' end. Even at the rate of ten solid hours of reading a day, with over fifty thousand books to tackle, their end, at best, can only be another's beginning.

SERVICE EXCHANGE

L EAVING THE MILITARY WAS A TOUGH DECISION FOR me, a decision that, I could tell, would come back and haunt me. Similar to a "vote to leave" for Britain's exit from the European Union, it could be best described as driven by ambition, imbued with fear. I was even apprehensive that life would never be the same again.

On my final trip to Pakistan just before my retirement from the military, I sat down with Dad. Our conversations for some time had been reduced to all things old. Apparently, one can never really tell how lonely people feel until they talk. The endless flow of words, memories, and embedded charm of his expression were all very engaging.

He started off, "Do you remember how you joined the military?"

I shook my head in the negative.

"Well, you were declared unfit in the initial medical exam. Weren't you?"

I recalled the faded memory of the scene. The

military doctor made me stand with heels locked. After a few minutes of deliberation, he ruled that I had knock-knee and was therefore unfit for military duty.

Before he could say anything more, I left the Military Hospital without collecting my documents. Joining the army had been a bumpy road, with ups and downs all along the way. One day I could imagine myself in uniform. Another day it appeared to be a distant dream. I had celebrated my recommendation from the Inter Services Selection Board and was already fancying myself as an officer when the doctor came to his premature conclusion. I could not find anyone to blame for it.

Weeks later, a clerk from the office called home. My mother picked up the phone. Somewhat sympathetic to my case although his knowledge of what occurred was limited to documents on record from my visit and from having seen me storm out of the office, the clerk convinced my mother that if I filed for an appeal, the doctor's opinion could be challenged. Without consulting me, my mother confirmed to the clerk that he should book a medical re-examination for me on the coming Monday. Little did she know that on my way back from the medical exam in Lahore, I would drop in at Government College Lahore, the country's prime university. I had walked in with the intent to enroll, but misfortune had probably not left me yet. Hours of waiting could only get me the old clerk, who peeped around the counter to tell me that admissions were closed and I could come back next year.

Before leaving the clerk's window, I wrote a note for the vice chancellor. (The college had recently acquired a vice chancellor along with its status change to a university.) In my hand-written letter, I not only narrated my account of the day but also embedded my stress, the suffocating August heat of the moment, and the unfairness of fate. I suggested the vice chancellor not deny me the opportunity to explore my abilities and make this world a better place with my spirit. I remember leaving the college premises with the certainty that no one would ever deliver the letter. The whizzing sound of the fan brought me back.

Dad was also lost in thought, but his face shone with nostalgia. He picked up the story.

"I received a call from the university. The vice chancellor had read your note and surprisingly decided to meet the young man who had the audacity to write directly to the pinnacle of power at the institution. A staff administrator had scheduled a meeting with you for Monday. Now on a single day, you had to appear for a medical board review and meet the vice chancellor for a probable admission offer, all at nine o'clock in the morning in two places that were almost an hour apart. We all sat down around the dinner table. Your mother was convinced that you had a chance with the military, and I was of the opinion that you should go and see the vice chancellor. You were, at best, indecisive."

I remember that we agreed Dad should go to the university for the meeting with the vice chancellor, and

I would go to the medical exam. On Monday morning, my father and I reached Lahore and parted ways for our respective destinations, only to see each other at five o'clock in the evening.

At the hospital, the doctor was two-hours late, but it was the pre-mobile age and I could not communicate this to Dad. I passed the time, cracking my knuckles.

"When I reached the university, the vice chancellor called me in after a few minutes of waiting." Dad recalled every detail of the story.

"There was this Victorian air about the place. The VC remarked that he was moved by the letter and had arranged admission for you. But when he heard you were considering another option, he told me that the university could not wait. I left the campus a dejected man and walked to Data Sahib."

Data Sahib is the shrine of the holy saint Ali al-Hajveri, believed by locals to be the guardian saint of the city of Lahore. Regardless of how faith and reverence contradict traditional teachings of Islam, this place had been a source of comfort for my father ever since he was orphaned at the age of four.

"I sat there at the shrine and started thinking of how the dream of my son could come crashing down. Some divine intervention had to happen. I got up to leave but was called by the caretaker. He said he needed my help in emptying the donation boxes and taking stock of the day's donations. I was initially hesitant, for it had always been a job restricted to a few chosen people trusted by the management. Although I was a regular visitor, I did not qualify for this 'honor.' I followed the caretaker to the inner compound where all the boxes were emptied. We sorted the bills and stacked them in order. It was already five o'clock when I handed him over the collection. While walking out, a prayer left my heart. For the service that I had done to the saint, he should probably move the divine system in your favor."

I could now relate the contentment writ large on Dad's face when he arrived to meet me at the railway station that day, 15 years earlier. Before I could tell him the news, he knew that something good awaited him. The military doctors had declared me fit, and I was all set to join the military academy two weeks later.

The call for prayer disrupted our recollections and conversation. He invited me to join him at the mosque. I had my reasons. He walked alone after telling me the following anecdote.

"An astronaut sent a message to ground station. 'I have reached outer space but cannot feel God.' Someone replied: 'Once you run out of oxygen, you will not only feel him but will meet him, too.'"

GEOGRAPHICALLY
DISTURBED

THE OUTWARD SIGNS OF THE GEOGRAPHICALLY DIS-
turbed are evident. As individuals, they suffer from
frequently recurring wanderlust and possess an insatiable
curiosity to explore the unknown. They are kindred
spirits to those who cherish as their family tangible and
intangible property worldwide. Common habits within
this eclectic group include a propensity to horde maps,
treasure high-performance carry-on bags, and cultivate a
lust for majestic scenery. They love establishing the connection between historical coincidences and can hold
court forever with people from unique traditions.

I never realized I was part of this larger collective
or that my condition was nameable. I heard the term
"geographically disturbed" for the first time while
ordering "free-women dumplings" and Dushanbe lamb
at a restaurant specializing in Central Asian cuisine.
An Italian friend was describing his peripatetic journey

between South America, South Asia, and Europe in pursuit of high-stakes business opportunities while I tried to make sense of a menu that was way too extensive for my dinner-hour attention span. I appreciated the distraction from the listings.

"I am geographically disturbed," he confessed.

"As in ... *disturbato*?" I inquired.

"Yes," he clarified.

Not that there was any nuanced difference between the English equivalents for the Italian – bothered, troubled, disturbed, inconvenienced, suffering from an ailment – but I wanted to be sure he and I were using the same terms as a basis for translation. "I, too, must be geographically *disturbata*," I thought, but said nothing.

A day earlier, a Pakistani graduate of the largest technical institute of Italy shared his theory. He had been a Ph.D. Research Fellow at Massachusetts Institute of Technology, two-time scholarship recipient, CEO in his own right, and social innovator. The world was divided in two, he confided: those who travelled and those who did not. He had no room for gray. Then, too, I masked my wholehearted embrace of his unsolicited comment to avoid revealing the extent to which it validated decades of my life.

A unique factor of being geographically disturbed is that the condition is self-inflicted. We, who are affected in this way, do not know how to live life otherwise. We take the risks along with the rewards, and bear the pain of separation along with the constant drain of nostalgia for people and places we ultimately must leave behind. We thrive on the enrichment and never tire in our search for more. We are always packing up part of what we just unpacked. We live in the very real realm of geography, where virtual and physical worlds constantly meet. The knowledge we gain only reaffirms the immensity of what we still need to discover. We are disturbed, *disturbati*, inconvenienced by an unquenchable thirst.

In the same week that two travelosophers confided in me their terms of engagement with the world, I coincidentally (?) read an online news report about an Italian marathon runner separated for ten days from the other runners during a sandstorm in the middle of a foot-race across the desert of northern Africa. He survived the ordeal on a diet of his own urine, bat blood, and determination. Eight more Saharan marathons and one divorce later, the former Olympic athlete is now planning his run for next year – from Morocco to Egypt through the desert.

Join the club of the geographically disturbed, where the thirst is as figurative as it is literal.

BOXED MEMORIES

I N ONE OF THE BOXES, FATIMA'S STUFF WAS PACKED. What an awful accumulation of junk that had gone down with so many years spun around it. The box contained the Monopoly® currency that had taken Fatima and me long hours to stack as I taught her how to differentiate amongst the fifty and one hundred rupee bills for the game. She learned the name of properties like Mayfair and Regent Street much before she realized that London would be our home one day, not out of admiration for the places but by sheer rote from frequency at the Monopoly® board. She was quick at the uptake, and the incidentals were her improved results in arithmetic.

In another box sat Fajr's Play-Doh® and all her colored pencils. Initially, I decided to trash them and started tossing until I reached for the pencil that had been sharpened almost a quarter of the way during my demonstration to her on the functioning of a sharpener. The decision to keep the memories intact was tough but not worth sacrificing for the sake of space, so I removed all the thrown-out pencils from the bin, put them in one bag, and sealed it. With this, Fajr's childhood in Pakistan was also sealed.

The Urdu books were packed together in another carton. I had bought these books at literature festivals across the country with the hope that one day my kids would speak the finest diction of our national language. They will now speak the finest diction of another, more international language.

One box held souvenirs from various cities around the Atlantic – London, Paris, Venice, Geneva, and Philadelphia. The small made-in-China magnetic monuments had been the source of much pre-purchase deliberation as I considered the converted cost in Pakistani rupees against the image each item would project while shining off the fridge back home.

My military uniform badges, shoulder titles, ranks, and name plates were jumbled together in the empty case for cufflinks. A story of struggle underlay every piece of insignia, spanning weeks, months, if not years. The Pakistan Army Command and Staff College badge that, at one point, appeared worth a life to me now occupied a corner of the velvet-lined walls of the case. I remember how I had cried the whole night in a dark room when I did not qualify for the final list of successful candidates in 2010. The next year, when I finally passed the entrance exam, life had altogether new meanings. Sitting at the airport lounge on the way to the College in Quetta, I ridiculed my thoughts of leaving the military, joking with my wife: "Do you remember, we once considered leaving a country like ours. How foolish of us." Fooled we were in the short-run, by the fallacy of our own decisions.

Every box was a time machine that took me to unanticipated zones of a time warp. Fatima's school records, Fajr's drawings from nursery school, empty lunch boxes and toys from visits to McDonald's®, my files of official correspondence, and photocopied notes from my wife for her fellowship exams all fit snugly into khaki-colored cartons, once home to chips and biscuits.

The movers have only just arrived, and I am already as nostalgic as an octogenarian veteran on Victory Day.

BANGLES,
LESSON ONE

SCRAMBLING TO ARRIVE IN COUNTRY WITH THE ability to say, at a minimum, "please" and "thank you" in Urdu, I found a Pakistani diaspora professor stateside who was willing to walk me through a few basic language lessons to cushion my communication landing abroad. Among key vocabulary words in lesson one – out of the grand total of three rushed lessons I was able to squeeze in – was the Urdu word for *bangles*. Incorporation of this term in lesson one seemed odd.

For a standard first-tier of vocabulary to be kept in the back pocket of the English learner I could imagine far more utilitarian words, such as *bank, restaurant,* or *newspaper.* References to accouterments, such as *pinky ring* or *ear cuffs,* would remain off-limits for many chapters to come. Jewelry, as a lexical subset, is not considered to be a first line of linguistic defense when travelling abroad.

What I had not yet realized in lesson one of three was the extent to which bangles for women constituted an element of attire in a category unto itself. Bangles in Pakistan are ubiquitous, demonstrating that language serves as a primer to culture in general. And though regional variations govern design styles, prevalence is a uniformity of cause. Bangles of glass and glitter compete for women's attention with bangles from China and Afghanistan. Bangles for the young may sparkle. Bangles for the seasoned intentionally distract. All coexist peacefully on the market.

During the traditional holidays of the Islamic calendar, shoppers and banglosphere converge at outdoor stands that brim with jingle-jangle for the femaledom of the nation. Dangling bangles lining the tops of kiosks catch the gleam of light, while between mobile vending carts they delineate boundaries. Long strands of tiny baby bangles link together like endless colored key rings whose combinations of five or six bracelets each lend coherence to separate series.

A brimming selection of bangles can find a home among general clutter in the open market, but surplus storage in the home is more of a challenge. The average collection of an adult woman could require a space of some ten to fifteen Slinkys® aligned horizontally. Unlike the metal spring toy, where all subsequent hoops in the sequence are pulled along to follow the spiral movement of the first circular form, individual bangle batteries can bring together twenty-six unconnected pieces, making accountability for the straying of loose hoops a question of lost hopes.

Throughout Pakistan, bangles add a signature touch to local femininity and are a reminder of how women can add coquetry through color to all tasks, however arduous.

While the official Government of Pakistan website lists jasmine as the national flower, mango as the national fruit, and the markhor (a mythical-looking unicorn-deer with twisted horns that inhabits the mountainous ridges) as the national animal, there is no mention of what is clearly the national accouterment of choice for women: the bangle.

FIRST DAY

I T WAS MY FIRST DAY.... SEPTEMBER 26, 2016. NO I don't think so.

It was my first day at London School of Economics and Political Science, and the first class was by Dr. Shakuntala Banaji, Program Director for Media, Communication and Development. Professor Banaji, I later realized, was a communication guru. She knew the very best of it: what to talk, how candid to get, and when to put one's foot down. So that was the first day, sitting with a class whose average age was less than the number of years I had spent in the military.

Shaku, as the professor preferred being called, had developed an interesting format for student introductions. Pairs of students sitting next to one another would each introduce the other to the class. I smiled and introduced myself to the girl sitting next to me.

Tatyana, who sat next to me, was as German as any German could get, strictly matter-of-fact and truly precise. I thought I had quite a lot of versatility in my profile, but it took her 2 minutes, 38 seconds, and 4 half-liners to sum up a life that I had taken almost a quarter of a century to build. Slowly and gradually the room filled up with the lives and times of people across the world.

The first day ... but it was not even close to what I had experienced my real first day. My *first* first day was April 1, 1994, the day I left my home to join Pakistan Air Force College Sargodha – a boarding school, to say the least – and never really returned.

Years later when Ammi, my mother, was nearing her death, my father told me in detail what had actually happened the night prior to my first day. On March 31, 1994, I was too excited to sleep, but then got tired and fell into deep sleep. Dad woke up in the middle of the night to find Ammi standing by my bed, crying. My father tried to calm her, something he never learned how to do during her lifetime. He explained that it was just a matter of a few days when I would be back for the summer break. For a moment, Dad recalled, Ammi's eyes shone with happiness until she asked, "But he will go back to school after the break?"

"Yes. In fact, this is his last night at our home," my father replied. "From now on, he will only come home for vacations."

It has been twenty-two years since that April 1, and I still yearn to define home.

The next morning, after the bedside chat between my parents, the mood was very festive. All of us packed into one car, driven by an uncle, and left for my new school. Dadi, my grandmother, had teary eyes and waved good-bye till the car turned. In the years to follow, every time I had to leave, Dadi would come down from her room, stand in the street, and wave me good-bye with tears in her eyes until I was out of her sight. It was her good-byes that I longed for, yet they boxed my heart.

After two hours, we reached Sargodha and were greeted by the school staff. It was a huge school, with vast playgrounds, imposing buildings, brick-lined pathways, trees planted sideways, and an independence of its own kind. Within an hour, I wanted my family to go back so I could start life on my own. As they wanted to stay, I had to comply.

A senior boy took us all to the mosque for Friday prayers and then for lunch. It was not until evening that the excitement of the place, newness of the clothes, and novelty of the independence had worn out. The bell for lights-out had silenced the dorm, barring an old ceiling fan that failed to air the moist bodies through the clogged gauze of mosquito nets.

An hour later, I started thinking about what Ammi and Dadi might be doing, thoughts that would return during occasional bouts of loneliness. I heard a voice: "I am Usman. Who are you? Can you introduce yourself?" While the dorm-boy-in-charge would practically shout at us to quiet down, Shaku was altogether different in her collegial, "OK class. Enough of introductions. Let's start the course."

OBAMA'S TAILOR

I FIRST MET SARWAR MUSHTAQ, IN CIRCUMSTANCES that I now define as extremely cinematic. He is not just known for his aviary or exotic plant collection from across the world, but also the elaborate stories he tells, the characters he meets, and the impression he leaves on film students through his mentorship heavily influenced by a love of philosophy and the art of story-telling. Having travelled almost half of the world, he has collected two things: coffee mugs and plants.

On travelling, his definition is not restricted to checking in to famous places or passing through famed cities, but actually taking up residence for months, buying groceries and commuting on public transport for a deeper local feel.

Somewhere along the journey, he started appropriating things. Small meaningless objects: a discarded parchment, a couple of nails, an odd spoon, a wine glass, a fistful of earth, a bit of clothing, a plant cutting, and sometimes things of value.

Each object coexists with the others in his home, and each has a story. Stories from Japan, Afghanistan, African jungles, Utah mountains, beaches of Greece…. The list is almost endless. There is another side to this disorder. Whenever he leaves for a trip or an adventure, he picks two or three of these objects to carry with him. Usually they will be deliberately left behind in place of the next piece he picks up. So there is a spoon from Corfu, Greece, sitting at this very moment in a kitchen drawer at his closest friend Steven's in upper Manhattan; and a shoe that a little girl left behind in Gruyères, Switzerland, in front of the Giger Museum, now adorning the foot of a young refugee in Jalozai camp on the Afghan border; while an ashtray from Lyon sits in the home of an elephant mahout in Sri Lanka. The only items that do not leave the house are mugs.

All the mugs that line his kitchen counter and the overhead cabinet have a personality, a history and, to top it all, a rich story to tell. The journey of these mugs to his kitchen is no less eventful than the other objects that fill and unfill his life.

Sarwar Mushtaq's stories are always fantastical and reveal the diverse geography of human nature. One of his wild tales struck me in particular, however, as it defined Pakistani awe for Americans and human curiosity, in general, about strangers.

Waiting for his dinner, SM, as I call him, received a call from a member of his filming team who had gone to cover a wedding event. They were having an issue with some of the shots and wanted him to come and guide them for more experienced angles. Taking into account his twenty years in the United States, they cautioned him not to show up in a worn-out T-shirt and shorts.

Half-heartedly, SM dressed up in a suit and drove to the venue. The place was quite upscale and had four lawns. SM first checked lawn A, then went to B, then C, and eventually D. He could not find the team at any of the four lawns, so he decided to wait for them to show up. He entered lawn A. As luck would have it, he was just in time for someone to usher him to the food stall. He made a plate for himself and, before he could sit down and eat, he saw a group of five to seven people approaching the table. He offered to leave them the seat so that they could talk freely, but the family insisted that SM should stay. Then came the dreaded questions.

Boy: "Haven't seen you…. Are you from the bride's side?"

SM: "No, I am not."

Woman from the same group (a little embarrassed): "Sorry, you must be from the groom's side. Very sorry."

SM: "No, I am not from the groom's side either."

Boy: "Then…?"

SM (maintaining his calm): "I live in Washington, DC, and just landed a few hours ago. I was called by someone for a meet-up here, but I couldn't find the guy. Was feeling hungry, so I sat down for the food."

Another woman: "Quite bad at the New York airport."

SM: "Yes, the snow is real bad."

Boy: "So you work in New York."

SM: "No, I work in DC."

Young girl: "What kind of work?"

SM: "I am a tailor, but I work for one client only."

Girl (interest piqued now): "Your client must be a rich man."

SM: "Not exactly rich but, yes, he is quite famous."

Girl: "What does he do?"

SM: "Politics."

Girl: "His name?"

SM (laughing): "Barack Obama."

Now the group actually went into an involuntary "wow!"

SM, by this time, was still living the moment, and was playing up his general knowledge about the First Family and the White House.

Old woman: "Whom do you like most in the Obama family?"

SM: "Malia and Sasha. They are such adorable girls. Very well mannered. Very groomed."

Uncle: "And Obama's wife?"

SM: "Oh, Michelle. No. Most of the time, she is grumpy."

Young girl: "What is it that you just don't like about their household?"

SM: "Bo, the dog. Won't let me work peacefully."

By this time, a young girl stepped ahead and asked for permission to take a selfie. That was when SM realized that his stretch of the imagination had actually spun too far. Before he could say no, there were almost thirty selfie clicks, and people were keying in all variety of mobile uploads in a rush. One of the girls called over the wedding photographer, who had to abandon the bride and groom to take photos of the group with SM.

It was only when SM saw the excited girl, who had asked him questions and taken a selfie with him, whispering something into the bride's ear, that he got up and excused himself on the plea of dessert. He placed his plate to the side and briskly walked towards exit, hearing the hum of people talking about Obama's Pakistani tailor, and how much Obama still loved Pakistan.

IN SEARCH OF
A WEDDING[*]

THE INVITATION SAID EIGHT O'CLOCK IN THE EVENING, which is code for "do not even think about coming at this hour." That much, I knew. Even an arrival around eight thirty would be too early by local standards.

Pakistani weddings are an experience in sensory overload. No one who is given the opportunity to share in such an invitation should pass it up. Thus I suggested to a colleague arriving from abroad that she accompany me to this wedding and arranged for her name to be added to the guest list. She was quite willing. Her job involved cultural exchange, and she wanted to feel the other side of the equation direct-mode. I informed her in advance about customary wedding-wear so she could make the proper wardrobe adjustments to her suitcase.

---

[*] "In Search of a Wedding" was originally published in *Khabr o Nazar: U.S. Embassy Magazine News & Views,* in 2015.

"Wear something glitzy," I instructed her. "You cannot go wrong. There is no such thing as over-the-top in this context. If it glitters, chances are it is event-appropriate."

Either she was just not in the mood, or she did not take me seriously. My visitor preferred understatement and modesty. We would have to get by on the classic foreigner's dispensation, a global opt-out that has come through for me on many occasions.

I worried about jetlag. My guest was operating on a time zone almost half a day behind Pakistan standard time. During most of the workday, like the rest of us who must roll into work following a pre-dawn flight arrival, she was muddling through the balancing act of fatigue and an inordinate workload. The night hours were sure to catch up with her. That is when collapsing from exhaustion becomes privately unavoidable. So I planned for us to be at the wedding premises at nine o'clock. This would assure she left her lodging quarters before she realized she was running out of residual energy.

Dropped off at the wedding hall site in our finery and not-so-finery, I observed the ominous darkness of the whole area – certainly nothing to tip off a passer-by about the likelihood of a wedding taking place anywhere on the extensive grounds.

The signboard outside the most likely spot for our wedding listed several names, none of which matched the fancy cursive script on the wedding invitation. The hall was dark, as were the other wedding halls concentrated in that area. Chairs were stacked up in mounds of six-to-ten high. It looked more like a wedding after-the-fact, once the guests had gone home.

We turned away and headed for the one building that did have lighting and a signboard indicating it was reserved for administrative matters. Inside, the administrator looked and acted more like an interrogator, asking me what I had come in search of.

"A wedding," I replied.

Granted, that was a silly answer. All anyone did within half a mile around me was plan, participate in, or attend weddings. This entire zone was reserved for weddings.

The administrator demanded to see my invitation card. He then inspected the card as if it could not possibly have been destined for me. I thought about the total lack of glitter and embroidery of my colleague, and wondered if that was a give-away for which I should feel guilty. I decided to stand firm as not guilty, and whipped the invitation card out of the pseudo-interrogator's hand. Either there was a wedding registered in his files under the said name, or not. Grilling me would get us nowhere.

The wedding hall administrator, who doubled as a mock intelligence-gathering agent, pointed to the darkened hall whence we had come and mumbled something incoherent eyeing his door for our exit.

At that point, I decided I did not care whose wedding we attended. We walked over more gravel in our fancy and not-so-fancy shoes to our starting point. There was a stir of activity and light at the far end of the hall where, previously, there was nothing but darkness and stacked chairs. We were in search of a wedding – any wedding – and were determined to attend one, whether or not we knew the bride and groom.

"Let's go in," I told my guest from abroad, who looked surprised that we would actually follow through with the idea of crashing a wedding. "We are in search of a wedding, and it looks like one is in the works here," I consoled her.

As we made our way through set-up crews prepping the hall despite the late hour, a young man rushed to our side. He introduced himself as the bride's brother and welcomed us to the function. Out of disembodied curiosity, I asked who was getting married.

Miraculously, the bride and groom turned out to be the protagonists whose names were embossed on the invitation card I almost lost to the hands of a wedding hall complex interrogator.

LOTS OF MANY
LANGUAGES

PAKISTAN IS A LAND OF POLYGLOTS, REINFORCED BY strong regional identities that run deep. A typical university graduate in Pakistan speaks at least three languages, having passed from mother tongue, to a language of instruction, to an imposed language envisioned to solidify a sense of nationhood through linguistic uniformity.

English, in addition to being an official language of the country, enters the psyche through higher education and the social preference for upward mobility. Urdu, the second official language, cuts across ethnic and tribal divisions as a lingua franca spoken by a majority of the population. But the bond resting closest to the heart is associated with the language predominating in each geographic region. These languages – the outward expression of ethnic identity – gain ground in new locations by following the trail of the internally displaced who en masse assure continuity of linguistic cohesion far from the sourceland.

"There are lots of many languages. Every thirty kilometers the language changes," a driver informed me. As a professional behind the wheel, he ought to know. He has been traversing the country's linguistic belts for years.

Even as Punjabi, Sindhi, Pashto, Saraiki, or Balochi enter the Urdu blender, residual nuances of origin remain. The panoply of regional color, a source of pride for the individual, provides opportunity for engagement on a more intimate cultural level and is the fodder behind my tale of introductory Punjabi pleasantries.

In need of someone who could turn out a few quick floral arrangements, I met a Punjabi flower vendor street-side not far from my neighborhood. He had severely truncated English skills but a keen ability to divert the attention of passers-by. Once potential customers stopped to listen, he would lure them closer to the flowers springing from a lineup of blue plastic buckets outside his shop. With mastery of less than a handful of words in English, he walked me toward a tidy row of buckets containing yellow and pale-orange long- and short-stem roses. Interested in doing business with him, I entered the stall, prepared for limited conversation and an excess of discovery. The shop owner pointed to a chair. Dutifully, I sat down.

My first job at age sixteen had been in a flower shop, where I incidentally learned the expression to be paid "under the table," as my tender age and illegal employment status required. I also retained, ever since, an appreciation for how single stems turn into colorful, sculpted displays.

The flowers I had admired outside the shop were yellow and pale-orange. Through gesticulation to owner and employee alike I requested a prevalence of these two colors in the arrangements I needed. They would be welcoming tones for my dinner guests later that evening. The owner nodded and relayed the information to his assistant in a language they shared.

In no time the floral technician gathered from different buckets the raw materials for turning concept into reality. He worked from a squatting position a few inches above the stone floor and surrounded himself with a palette of red roses, pink alternates, and green filler – all of which resembled little my request. He maintained an agile grip on a small clipper, the only tool he used to guard against thorns. His movements were swift and skilled.

As the arranger stuck stems into water-soaked pincushions, the series of three floral sculptures took on increasing presence and dimension. The pieces were moving in the right direction – if not in color, certainly in form. Although I was hesitant to interrupt progress, in reverse gesticulation I decided to point out the discrepancy between the bucketed flowers outside and the red- and pink-headed flowers strewn all over the floor inside.

"No flowers. Your color."

A highly practical man, the shop owner was not about to lose a sale over such minor details. There were simply not enough flowers in my preferred colors. Rather than suffer the fuss of a discussion, he had decided to proceed with the arrangements according to the flowers he had on hand and in quantity. I admired his bold pragmatism.

The skilled hands of the craftsman and the personality of the shop-owner passed the time. I was offered tea and a soft drink. I politely refused. It hardly seemed appropriate for me to be consuming bear-bones resources that could quench the thirst of either of these two gentlemen in the stagnant hot air of the shop. The owner wasted no time insisting. Off went the soft-drink bottle cap, and he took a swig.

He told me he had five children. All attended a local madrassa for free Islamic religious instruction. It was important to him that I knew he had a family of a respectable size and that he was from the Punjab. He taught me the words for "thank you" in his native Punjabi, then tested me over and over until the three mini-centerpieces were complete and I could say "thank you" to him, naturally, in his language of choice.

The assistant carefully placed the centerpieces in my trunk on top of week-old newspaper scraps rescued from the recesses of the shop to help absorb the extra water supply now oozing slowly from the pincushions' interior. I stepped on the accelerator to take care of a last errand before sunset, conscious of the newspaper sheets' diminishing shelf life.

Whatever languages were spoken at the gas station where I found the air pump for car tires, English was not among them. I pressed my shoes hard against the tires, scissored my hands back and forth to demonstrate air "all gone," and pointed to the air pump. Everyone but the tire attendant was perplexed by the charades.

The four tires were dangerously low on air. I was relieved to finally complete the task. To wrap up the transaction with the attendant, I gestured to the tires, then displayed the global "how much" with my two palms open. I knew there was no fixed amount for such a service, but I inquired anyway out of respect.

"Your happiness," he responded, and flicked a single palm sideways and upward to underscore the open-endedness of what might come of the suggestion.

His rudimentary word choice, rich in poetry, did in fact seal my happiness, inspire my generosity, and confirm how proficient consummate polyglots can be at putting to strategic use limited vocabulary.

HOME

THE HEAVY EASTERN EUROPEAN ACCENT OF THE airhostess implied that she made no attempt to conceal it. English had become a language of all accents.

"Welcome home," she said as the aircraft came to a complete halt, sending me riveting onto memory lane. What exactly had become home for me? How to define home?

The Malaysian mother-daughter duo seated next to me asked if England was my home. I hesitantly moved my head north-south, and an envy descended into their expressions. I then said "no," followed by a confused "I don't know." But they could not be bothered much with my existential doubts, as they had only one day for sight-seeing in London before flying to other tourist destinations across the channel.

For a yes, England was my home, it had been about six months since my family and I had moved here. Already I could tell that my children would have more of England in their collective memory than Pakistan. For a no, the country of our most recent move would always question whether my kind of diversity exerted a positive or negative influence on society, ever skeptical of our intentions. In cities throughout England I still drive fearing that every car is chasing me for violating some traffic rule. I also wear an apologetic smile and act extra polite to locals, which tells them – and me – that I do not belong. Even the sense of being just-one-in-the-crowd, rising from the underground elevators, continues to haunt me and will do so for a long time to come. And although corruption, injustice, and inequality reign supreme in my homeland, I will always miss its air of acquaintance. So what exactly breeds homesickness?

Whereas I used to feel alienated from the culture of my heritage during my days in Pakistan, as I grow older, I will somehow start yearning for it, not realizing that, by then, I will have adapted to the culture of this kingdom.

The smiling faces of Brits from different walks of life that adorn the entrance walls of the tunnels connecting the aircraft to the terminal, greet visitors with the magical word in the text beneath: "Welcome." Across turbaned heads, South Indian faces, and European-dressed passengers, I was thinking how this two-home phenomenon affects people from Southeast Asia more than any other part of the world. In Sind, the seat of ancient civilizations and now a province in Pakistan, the saying goes that a Sindhi's homesickness starts the moment he exits the gates of his house. So what essentially qualified as home for me?

My father was born in the gossiping town of Shah-dara, on the outskirts of Lahore, where people could live without food but not without the juicy tales of how others' lives went on, and who did what with whom. The people of this town refused to mind their own business. In fact, their only business was the other's business. It might well have been my home, too, but then my grand-father was murdered, and my grandmother was left as insecure as a young widow could be. She migrated along with her three young daughters, her only son, and a couple of suitcases to Lyallpur, another coming-of-age-city in the province. Years later, when the government tilted in favor of the Kingdom of the House of Saud, the city was renamed Faisalabad.

Planned by the officers of the British Raj under the White Man's burden, the city was largely a trader's set-tlement. Although Lyallpur/Faisalabad gave my father everything, it could never qualify as home for him. It was here that he went to primary school, joined a col-lege, made best friends, married my mother, raised his children, and built his two homes – one after another. It was here that he graduated from being a clerk to a successful businessman. But now and then, whenever he spoke of home, he was referring to Shahdara.

As for me, I was probably as homeless as divinity could foretell. I was born in Faisalabad but never really liked it. For the sake of quality education, I left there when I was thirteen, never staying in any one city for more than two years from then on. Besides a decent civi-lized hairstyle, a career in the military and its associated wanderings also took away my very sense of home.

Before I could settle down somewhere, my posting orders disconnected me from being able to establish a place to call home. All that remained with me from my previous posting stations were a few friends and acquaintances from the grocery store or forged during long waits at the auto repair shop. Every now and then they would pop up on my contact list.

The immigration officer asked me my reason for visiting England. All I could tell him was that it was my new home.

A verse from Matthews echoed in my head.

"And Jesus said to him, the foxes have holes, and the birds of the air have nests, but the Son of man has not where to lay his head."

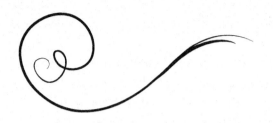

YOUR TIME IS THE
RIGHT TIME

I T IS ALWAYS THE SAME. YOU HAVE TO ASK, OBSERVE, get it wrong a few times, before getting it right. Time is not a concept shared by all equally, everywhere. It may take several forays into experience until local conventions of time and time management are made clear. Punctuality runs along a sliding scale of no universally held value. The sooner you grasp that, the less time spent in perplexity. Though even the concept of soon is circumscribed by circumstance and by the country in which the soon-ness is due to expire.

Within the 450 square miles of Islamabad Capital Territory, the notion of time can elicit different interpretations based on the occasion. Punctuality for prayer has no comparable equivalent to the understanding of timelines required – or not – for a meeting, performance, or wedding. A "timely" start of an event may also depend upon the arrival of a chief guest or key figure lending validity to the gathering.

At a youth-intensive multimedia event where my arrival on the scene was not envisioned as part of the official program, I was told five times in a period of ninety minutes that the event would begin "in fifteen minutes." Initially believing what I was told, I came to understand that the offering of a time-frame for the ceremony to begin was meant as a comforting pleasantry, as you might tell someone you will be back in a few minutes, never intending to create a literal expectation of a one-hundred-and-eighty-second turnaround on your return time.

Jokingly and to put my hosts at ease about the time generously elapsing, I shared with those in the waiting area of the principal's office my understanding that the promised fifteen-minute interval need not be taken literally. A school administrator took great offense at the comment, insisting that Pakistan adhered to international standards of time. Following another forty-five-minute wait of "fifteen minutes" before the inaugural ceremony got off the ground, I wondered why my good-natured remark had landed backwards. I made a mental note to avoid in the future all jokes about time.

When another large-scale high school event by a different host began two-and-a-half hours late despite the attrition rate among the high-level foreign dignitaries invited to attend, I took a deeper interest in deconstructing the seeming contradictions in perceptions of time and timeliness.

In an off-hand conversation with a driver from out of town about weddings and how difficult it can be to get the bride's and groom's caravans to arrive punctually at the ceremonial festivities, I finally gained the insight I was seeking about the relativity of timeliness in this new cultural context.

"In Pakistan, anything can happen," the driver explained.

Among so many vehicles and so few comprehensive vehicle maintenance checks throughout the year, inevitably someone's car will have a flat tire along the way, causing the full wedding-bound caravan to come to a complete halt. A child in one of the cars will then become sick, and the bathroom stop en route for the ladies will cause additional delays. By the time the two travelling parties arrive at the wedding site, each having supported the inconveniences of the other passengers in order to undertake the entirety of the journey together, the event start time printed on the invitation is rendered irrelevant.

Given the hard work and financial sacrifice that goes into celebrating a wedding plus the group effort sustained in physically reaching the ceremony venue in unison as a gesture of solidarity toward the bride, the groom, and their respective sides of the family, "whenever you arrive," my interlocutor summed it up, "is the right time. *Your* time is the right time."

SACRED SETS OF FOUR

I HAVE TAKEN TO SIMPLIFYING MY LIFE. ONE-POT meals, coordinated errand runs, limits on incremental wardrobe expansion that are in direct proportion to the amount of available closet space. The goal is to downsize the mundane, freeing up time for more creative endeavors.

Over-simplification does not come naturally, though, as my thinking patterns are far from inherently linear. My mind tends to sweep up everything in its path, processing the end simultaneously with the beginning. As a coworker once remarked rather perceptively, my inbox and outbox are the same. I actually take notes to keep up with myself. Under such circumstances, simplification is complicated.

As 2015 was coming to a close, much of my time and energy was consumed in following political developments in Haiti. My job on the Haiti Desk required real-time tracking of events unfolding, despite holidays and weekends. Haiti was gearing up for National Day as well as the final round of a three-part election cycle that, in the end, did not make it into the 2015 almanac. In addition to the end-of-year holiday rush, I was co-planning a trip to Haiti whose dates were edging near coincidence with the reconfigured electoral calendar. The more the country's electoral calendar slipped, the more its institutional future and my vacation plans threatened to intersect paths.

I was overextended and certain to miss a beat. Something was bound not to capture my timely attention. As a strategy to avoid forgetting to pay the rent on my apartment before leaving the country for Haiti, I decided to pay two months of rent at once. It was a reductivist approach to a task list in crescendo. One less item for the check-list.

Paying rent in my apartment building is simple. Tenants place the monthly rent check into a drop box that looks much like a U.S. Post Office mail slot. I remember one day thinking how easy it would be to mistake the mail chute for the rental payment chute, although that fleeting thought lost out to others in the bubbling sea that is my head. Gone, as if down a parallel chute.

With two completed rent checks in hand, I alighted from the apartment complex elevator early one morning. *Whoosh!* down the slot sailed the checks. In the instant they left my hand I also realized that I had deposited them through the wrong slot, into the United States Postal Service (USPS) mail chute that Wikipedia describes as a "largely defunct letter collection device" but in my building is fully operable and managed by men and women in USPS uniforms, not by apartment management administrators looking for monthly rental payments. I had done the unthinkable. My checks, two months in advance, were now to be lost in a jumble of neighborhood mail then dumped at a central collection point for sorting. The proverbial rent-check in a haystack hit home hard, and simple was becoming rapidly complex.

When I called the United States Postal Service Customer Service line, the representative confirmed that the whereabouts of my checks was a lost cause, less traceable with each passing moment. He strongly suggested I cancel the checks. My call to the banker, at least, was more positive. Taking pity on my clumsiness, she extended to me the Single Act Idiocy Waiver, charging for one canceled check though she should have charged me for two. The loss of dignity was a small price to pay for waiver of the double cancellation fee.

That night, I wrote out two more checks and placed them in the rent check deposit slot immediately. I was proud to have taken swift corrective action.

The next day via email, the building administrator informed me that the payment amount in numerals and the amount in words on both checks did not match, and asked me to reissue the two checks so that everything lined up. I not only introduced a new error but faithfully reproduced it in two prepaid monthly installments.

Granted, I was overworked. Still, I should have been able to summon minimal concentration to succeed in this routine task. Frustrated by my own obtuseness, I drew lines through the offending checks and wrote two new checks – now on the third set in my thinning checkbook.

The next morning I slipped two new checks into the correct deposit slot.

Another email pinged me midday, from the building administrator. I thought it would be confirmation of the rent payment. But no, there was another clerical mis-step. I had written the amount of money in the PAY TO THE ORDER OF field and filled in the company's name under AMOUNT.

"Unprecedented," was my one-word response in an email back to the apartment building administrator. I thought about the fourth attempt to pay rent that awaited me in the evening when I returned home.

That night, I stared long and hard at the checkbook that had become my enemy, mustering more concen-tration than a twelve-hour workday cared to part with and infinitely more than such a menial task required. I paused before filling in each line, as if this were the first time I had ever written a check: month, day, and year for *DATE*; payment information under *AMOUNT*; com-pany name on the line for *PAY TO THE ORDER OF*. The monumental task of placing the two new checks into the correct slot I would save for the next morning.

An elder of the Aymara people from Bolivia once explained to me that four is a sacred number for many Native American nations throughout the Western Hemisphere: four directions of the wind, four colors of corn (white, yellow, blue/black, and red) plus the four seasons. I have incorporated this episode of extended mental blips into the pantheon of my memory-lapsing mishaps as the sacred set of four rental checks.

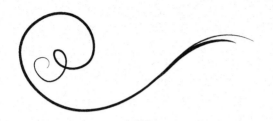

ONE TRIBE TO
ANOTHER

THE GARRISON CITY OF LAWTON, IN SOUTHWEST
Oklahoma, is an otherwise sleepy community. Like
almost all cantonments across the globe, it also sits far
and away from the cosmopolitan world of regional cap-
itals. The universally accepted wisdom for this distance
is to keep soldiers away from the civilian world, though
such a concept over time cannot sustain the want of real
estate developers who, with all their magic of marketing
and concrete, fill these gaps with housing projects at the
expense of the middle class.

At the time of my military student exchange program in Lawton, the town's only getaway besides a local
airport that served occasional flights and local amateur
pilots was the Comanche National Museum and Cultural
Center. During the first part of the program an attempt
was made to familiarize participants in the course with
local culture, so Comanche National Museum and

Cultural Center was a logical choice for our session on cultural awareness.

Standing in the main entrance to the museum, looking toward the "History and Culture" exhibit, I realized how Americans' sense of history is the reason behind their amazement at all things historical. I would often earn awe-inspiring looks upon mentioning to my classmates that I lived on a road that was 2000 years old. Only the Indian and Bangladeshi officers understood that it was not for the love of history but for the lack of town planning that Southeast Asians typically settled for accommodation on a historical location.

Comanche National Museum and Cultural Center presented the history of the Comanche Nation in a very appealing manner. While one part of the museum was dedicated to the dying culture of the Comanche Nation and its language, another paid tribute to Comanche servicemen. Known as the Code Talkers, these men were employed by the Allied Forces during World War II to send and receive secret messages using their native language, without fear of being deciphered. A few kilometers from the museum, a graveyard paid tribute to the Comanche servicemen who gave their life for the country by fighting alongside, and for, non-indigenous Americans.

The diversity index of our class was exceptionally high, given the defense and diplomatic relations of the United States, as were the number of questions regarding the origin, conflict, and existing status of the Comanche Nation.

Many of us were amazed at the whole question of

a federal government initially taking over the reservations, with states subsequently building museums to preserve the indigenous cultures the larger State sought to contain. Years from now when some of us rise in the hierarchy, we will comprehend the political cycle of peace, conflict, expansion, and governance.

Whatever happened between the American states and the Comanche people is a long trail of treaties, agreements, deceit, treachery, violence, and isolation. It is heavily shrouded in mystery, with each side claiming victory, both moral and physical. From the Treaty of Camp Holmes to the Jerome Agreement of 1892, the two sides have two very different versions of the whole affair, but this is probably why story makes up two-thirds of the word *history,* literally and figuratively.

The love, care, and commitment of the Comanche people to their roots left a profound impact on me. Within days, I read all the treaties between the American states and the Comanche Indian tribes. Of all the treaties, Medicine Lodge Treaty impressed me the most. Apart from its geo-political manifestation, the subtle anguish in the speech of the Comanche Chief was painfully poetic. My interest in calligraphy prompted me to write down a few excerpts from it and keep them in my diary. In fact, all that is left from my visit to the museum are my calligraphic excerpts of Medicine Lodge Treaty and a miniature souvenir baby cradle, fashioned after those used by the Comanche people.

The Comanche reference would time-travel me to

Pakistani tribal areas, already a famous place in the newsroom and U.S. information sphere.

During the morning review of current affairs, our class would often question the extent of authority exercised by the Pakistani government on its own tribal areas and the associated perception of terrorism in this rugged terrain, images courtesy of CNN and Fox News.

I would firmly advocate for the quasi-autonomy held by the tribal peoples of northwest Pakistan and would draw parallels to the same autonomy being proffered to the Comanche tribe, but the argument was often shot down by my American class-fellows, though politely. Somehow, it did not occur to them that the Comanche of Oklahoma were, deep down, identical to the Wazirs, Mehsoods, and Afridis of Khyber or Orakzai agencies in the federally administered tribal areas of Pakistan.

Time, which has its own geography, continued to take shape in the form of opinions and changing mindsets. I visited the tribal areas of my country in October of 2015. The place was no more the wild yet peaceful land that had existed in our national and individual memory. Its wilderness had become associated with aggressiveness due to frequent military campaigns against terrorists. Although the whole region was now being brought into the political and administrative mainstream, the surgery had left permanent scars.

Talking to a local, I heard of native Pashto poet Izzatullah Zawab and his popular poem. The verses reflected the emotive angle of political conflict and oppression.

Every time I would reread the poem, the feeling that I had read its content elsewhere strengthened. I decided to write out the poem long-hand, in calligraphy.

As I took out the binder of other calligraphic pieces, excerpts from the Comanche treaty fell out. The parallels were unmistakeable.

For the Conqueror*
Izzatullah Zawab

Dear friend, I admit that you have the authority on my life
You are powerful enough to grant me light or curse me
    to darkness
You snatched our mountains and land from us
And our brothers, and our friends
You imposed war on us and fired bullets at us
You took away our people and our Khyber
You took our faith and our heart, too
You took away the self-seeding wild flowers that blos-
    somed on our thatched roofs
No longer can we embrace the beautiful girls of our town
You took away our short-lived romances

---

*   English translation is by Muhammad Hassan Miraj, printed with permission by Izatullah Zawab.

Medicine Lodge Treaty

Comanche Chief *Parry-wah-say-men* (Ten Bears)

I know that you had come to do good to me and my people. The blue dressed soldiers and the Utes came from out of the night when it was dark and still, and for camp fires they lit our lodges. Instead of hunting game they killed my braves, and the warriors of the tribe cut short their hair for the dead. They made sorrow come in our camps, and we went out like the buffalo bulls when the cows are attacked. I was born on the prairie where the wind blew free and there was nothing to break the light of the sun. I was born where there were no enclosures and where everything drew a free breath. I want to die there and not within walls. So, why do you ask us to leave the rivers and the sun and the wind and live in houses? Do not ask us to give up the buffalo for the sheep. The Texans have taken away the places where the grass grew the thickest and the timber was the best. The white man has the country which we loved, and we only wish to wander on the prairie until we die. I want no blood upon my land to stain the grass. I want it all clear and pure and I wish it so that all who go through among my people may find peace when they come in and leave.

SEVEN SKETCHES

BEFORE I ARRIVED IN PAKISTAN, WHEN MY IDENTITY as far as future Embassy colleagues were concerned was still shrouded in the relative anonymity of a name embedded in an e-mail, speculation began to stir about my style as a boss. The sole source of insight was from a colleague who had met me physically on one occasion and with whom I shared an intervening distance of more than 1,400 miles over the years while we worked "together" from time to time on issues of mutual concern in the Dominican Republic.

As dearth would have it, and for lack of alternative sources, the single-source colleague became the resident expert. When asked by Embassy personnel in Pakistan what I looked like, she provided an easy-to-grasp response based on the little she knew. She told the staff that I looked a lot like another American officer who was already working in the section where I was assigned.

The thought was comforting to the rest of the staff. The promise of a familiar face required less adaptation to change and made for an easier transition to a new boss. For whatever reason during an evening's meandering conversation with my colleague, now that the 1,400 miles were reduced to three feet across a dinner table, I gave little importance to her mention of the similarity between C and me.

My first day at work in my new environs began a couple of days after our conversation and not long after the crack of dawn. The trans-Atlantic, trans-Gulf, and trans-Arabian flights resulted in wake-up times for days on end that were anyone's guess. I walked toward the building in the faint morning light with barely a soul around. As I approached the door to the office space, I felt the shadow of a tall, thin figure behind me, and two of us ended up reaching for the door handle at the same time. I looked up to hold the door open and let the person through. A mirror image met my gaze. There stood a woman of the same height, with the same build and a similar close-cropped hairstyle. My look-alike cut a lithe figure and wore a long, flowing scarf, much like my own flair for such wardrobe touches. The 1,400-mile colleague was right: there were now two versions of what had been one in the office.

Immediate confusion ensued. People I had never seen before would tell me about activities we had participated in together in Pakistan, prior to my arrival on the continent. A woman yelled after me so insistently from behind that I had to turn around, although I was certain it was not my name she was calling. Students had glowing reports about presentations I never gave, and foreign diplomats shared in-jokes about events I never attended. Now that there were two of us posing as one at the Embassy, people were uncertain whether they had met me, or my duplicate. In the office they joked about taking up a collection for DNA testing and placing bets on the results.

Like the problem, the solution was clearly visual. I invited my "other" to a photo op. We coordinated colors, so as not to clash, and chose a neutral background. She kicked off her heals to capture our matching height. The photo shoot began in seriousness but ended in silliness and laughter. It was absurd to think that I had travelled half way around the world to meet a co-national who looked like me.

The workers in the Embassy print shop laminated a wallet-size photo of "the twins." By their own admission, they only realized we were two different people when they saw us side by side, in the photo.

At the Embassy reception desk, a woman pulled me over. She looked worried and uncertain. She tested the waters by asking if there was someone else who looked like me and worked in the same Embassy compound.

I pulled the laminated photo out of my wallet.

"You mean this woman?" I asked. The receptionist smiled, relieved that it was not her imagination.

"We have seven sketches in life," she informed me. "Seven people in the world are our carbon copies. You have six more to find."

Figuring the concept might have its origins in early Pakistani legend, I looked up "seven sketches" on the Internet. I found instead a description of the collection Seven Sketches, by twentieth-century Hungarian composer Béla Bartók. The AllMusic critic called it a "two-faced work ... that looks forward and backward." The first piece in the collection is titled "Portrait of a Girl." Not just another coincidence, I presume.

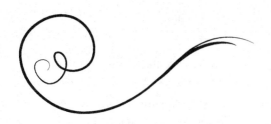

FIRST FAMILY
FOOD COURTS

D ALLAS HAD A NOSTRADAMUS MOMENT STRUC-
tured in a building. The French physician and seer
wrote a prophecy in 1555, labeled as 1 Q26.

The great man will be struck down
in the day by a thunderbolt,
The evil deed predicted by the bearer of a petition

After almost 455 years, I stood at the place that tes-
tified to his genius, according to some. On 22 November
1963, Lee Harvey Oswald stood in the window that
opened to the road and shot U.S. President John
Fitzgerald Kennedy. The bullet hit Kennedy at the spot
marked on the road with an X, and brought his presi-
dency to an abrupt end.

Despite the tradition in the East, where accidental
deaths give way to glorification, by all realistic anal-
yses, Kennedy is not granted this stature in the West. A

detailed visit to the Sixth Floor Museum in Dallas, Texas, ended all the charm that I had once associated with this iconic politician. The image of Jacqueline, adored above the fireplace of almost all who's who of the early 1960s, had caused the couple's over-glorification though later put straight by truthful history. Declassified documents tell us that despite Kennedy's charismatic personality, had he survived the assassination attempt, his chances of getting another term in office were quite low.

Probably headstrongness, a false sense of ego, and over-overconfidence take away the best of almost all the young leaders whose support derives from their charisma – be it the Kennedys in the United States or the Bhuttos in Pakistan.

The parallels are unmistakable. Kennedy rode the public stream of want for greatness in the sixties, while Zulfiqar Ali Bhutto took over the socialist slogan of Food, Shelter, and Clothing for All, in the populist politics of the same decade. Bhutto's rise to power was super quick, as was Kennedy's. Both had a glamorous first family, mixed reputation for pacifism and human right abuses, and both met a very tragic end. Yet people believe that each would have been saved by an early exit from politics, and the two are missed from the political sphere with a mix of emotion and nostalgia.

There was speculation about the assassination attempt on Kennedy's life, but the threat of death to Bhutto took another form.

A young superintendent of police called former

Prime Minster Bhutto and told him that there was a First Information Report (FIR) registered against him on charges of murder. A confident Bhutto, from the other side of the telephone line, laughed off the warning call. Little did he know the very same FIR would walk him to the gallows.

After visiting the museum in Dallas dedicated to the legacy of John F. Kennedy, I had lunch on the first floor of the building. Years later, the place in Rawalpindi where Zulfiqar Ali Bhutto was hanged was converted to a park, which now houses a McDonald's®.

PIGEON COURIER
NETWORK

I T HAD NEVER OCCURRED TO ME THAT A ROOFTOP view could reveal the existence of a parallel world. Looking out over minarets, blue plastic water reserve tanks, the haze of an early morning sun, and conical Hindu temple spires attesting to a population segment in Rawalpindi long since in decline, I see atop buildings everywhere open-air cages several stories high that, from afar, appear to contain birds.

The expertise of the two area guides who accompany me includes knowledge of how this historical satellite city came to be – changes within society that engendered new needs and developments that set the old ones to rest. My unending questions about the sites we stumble upon fall well within their sociocultural comfort zone, and they take pleasure in superimposing logic on the chaos around us. As the sun makes its way toward the zenith, the unbridled hum of human activity picks up swiftly.

After descending mismatched staircases back down to the street, I inquire about the birdcages, assuming the mirage to have been a product of the early morning haze and my inability to accurately describe this high-point metallic overlay.

"Pigeon pets," they tell me.

Pigeons in a cage on a hot summer day, when the breeze at that height moves freely through the grated side panels is a concept I can grasp. Caged birds trapped during the winter months, when the city is enveloped in darkness through dawn, paints a more somber picture.

Curios at street level capture my fancy and refocus my thoughts elsewhere. Tree trunks shoot through buildings and sacred spaces. Newsprint and stray magazine pages are stuffed into crevices between wood and pole to prevent choice words from falling to the ground. The community takes no chances that a pickup in the wind may land the papers in a pile of blasphemy on the pavement. An elderly couple outside a dwelling at the far end of an impasse claims the family has inhabited the spot for over two hundred years. In a tiny birdcage hanging from an eave outside the simple shelter, three cramped parrots are outfitted in pink- and orange-dyed feathers. The city's living history is humbling.

When I leave the inner maze, the maze does not leave me. Rawalpindi has gotten under my skin: too much humanity to push aside.

Weeks go by. The notion of pet pigeons in tall cages on rooftops far from the family life below still makes little sense. I delve further into the subject and learn that there are fraternities of pigeon lovers in country who train the short-neck birds as messengers. Capable of flying long distances between major cities, a trained messenger pigeon can identify the route back to home, even if the outbound journey is undertaken by car.

The number of cages visible from Rawalpindi rooftops now becomes more understandable. Pigeon courier services involve lucre. From pets to couriers, transference of innate pigeon skills toward new applications is keeping the fraternity of modern pigeon *wallahs* busy.

A 2012 media report recounts the launch by a telecommunications conglomerate of a "team of courier pigeons" to deliver messages around the country. The business plan seeks to fill the twenty-five percent network coverage gap in the country during periods when cell service is shut down for security reasons. Though it may be a spoof, there is practical sense in it. The year before, some twenty-five miles into India beyond the Pakistan-India border, a local resident turned in to the police station a suspected pigeon "spy" caught with a Pakistan telephone number and address among its feathers and a tiny rubber ringlet clipped around its ankle.

Over the centuries, "pigeon pets" prove to be a unique litmus test for and symbol of continuity in sub-continental relations and technology.

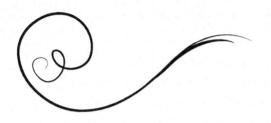

TALIBAN MONEY

I NEEDED A NEW TALISMAN, HAVING WORN DOWN THE *faux* silver bracelet to its copper underpinnings and taxed its stretched-out elastic innards through nonstop wear and tear. The hot season, in particular, had taken a toll, peeling back the hammered silver coating and forcing elastic into a final stretch.

In local markets, no replacement piece could be found for the all-purpose, neutral, and understated old-faithful I sought to decommission. The aging bracelet was diametrically opposed to prevailing costume jewelry taste in Pakistan. Chatting up vendors at open stalls and kiosks likewise failed to produce options from hidden reserves that might end my search.

I gave up and, on an aimless weekend morning, wandered along a line of shops, past window displays of elaborate jewelry for weddings and other life-changing events. A darkened showcase of Central Asian artifacts drew me closer for the mystique of the exhibit. The feel of history was written on every object in the display case, which featured deep-blue lapis lazuli-encrusted Afghani handiwork, antique glassware, and thick-rimmed jewelry.

I entered the store, where my eyes adjusted to even less light. The eclectic collection included czar-epoch teacups and Turkmen tribal wrist cuffs. A couple speaking Chinese maintained an animated exchange in a corner so cluttered, the subject of their concentrated interest was impossible to determine. Every shelf and segment of the store was filled. As I made out the definitions of a single object, items in the immediate vicinity would gain added visibility in the dim light.

On the accessories shelf, I sifted through heavy bracelets and brooches dotted with reddish-orange carnelian inlays, turquoise stones, and black semi-precious highlights that gave each piece a mark of dignity and individuality. The bracelets were wide and long, taking in with the wrist a sizeable portion of the lower arm. To wear one of these "armlets" was to possess the protective powers its intricate patterns were purported to exude. I tried on several to feel the uniqueness of a bracelet encasing so much skin.

The shopkeeper showed unusual patience, detecting my genuine fascination. I did not want him to lose customers on account of my indecision and suggested he approach the Chinese couple while I tried to make up my mind. Their area of the store had larger items and promised a heftier sale, but he confided in me that the two had visited the store many times before and never bought anything.

With difficulty, I decided on a silver pre-Soviet Tekke Turkoman bracelet with an imperfection that underscored its handmade nature. I tried to visualize the woman, from a nomadic Uzbek-Turkmen tribe, who had worn this geometric patterned bracelet before me. How vastly different we were, and yet I would carry forth her clan's legacy of protection in the form of handcrafted beauty.

As I laid out every last bill I had on me that day to secure the unexpected purchase, my eyes still wandered through the shop. Again, the shopkeeper – who had come to Pakistan by way of Afghanistan and even confessed to a group of relatives in New York – caught the spark of my curiosity and offered me more history.

From under the main display counter, where transactions took place through an improvised cash register, he took out a large transparent plastic envelope containing Russian rubles from the late-nineteenth and early-twentieth centuries. The highly ornate bills were of varying rectangular sizes. I spread them out on the counter to admire them more fully. The shop owner then placed an additional stack of bills on the glass counter.

"Taliban money," he pronounced.

The concept was astounding. Under Taliban rule, the Taliban Central Bank had declared the currency in circulation to be largely worthless and cancelled the extant Russian printing contract. That left the printing of Afghani banknotes up for grabs among a range of free-for-all sources, including counterfeiters. Externally the notes were devalued to over 20,000 Afghani to the U.S. dollar. Yet here, at this improvised payment counter some eighteen years later, a cross-border citizen was making money off of currency that, at one point in time, had been reduced to practically zero value.

My bracelet earned back every bit of legal tender I doled out for it by virtue of the tales it uncovered.

DOGS BEYOND
BORDERS

THE UNNAMED FRIEND HAD AN UNASSUMING PER-
sonality. He had climbed the four floors to reach
my apartment and was still trying to catch his breath.

Every now and then, he would drop in with an anecdote to remind me what an eventful life he had lived.

"My dad worked for the Public Works Department,
and he took us to places where people now go for either
tourism or jihad." He meant Karakoram Highway, in
the picturesque north of Pakistan, as well as Mohmand
Agency and Shawal, in the tumultuous tribal areas of the
country. Born in Sindh Province, in the southeast, his
parents hailed from Punjab, in the northeast, yet he had
lived in the northwest province of Khyber Pakhtunkhwa
for most of his life, giving him a connection with almost
every part of the country.

"I left my house for jihad when I was in eighth
grade," he recalled.

"That was before you passed your tenth grade?" I asked.

"Yeah. If this is the chronology they still follow," he remarked sarcastically.

"And then?" Interested, through a borrowed understanding of jihad from the West, I prodded him on.

"Nothing. Since most of my friends came from tribal areas, it was more of a teenage adventure.

"We actually wanted to avenge Murtaza Bhutto for his hijacking of the Pakistani International Airlines flight, but when we reached Kabul, we forgot the name of his organization and returned after four days and three Indian films. We were taken to the police so often that they refused to continue taking down our names for the record, with the police commissioner asking his subordinates: 'Are these the only miscreants in the capital?'"

Somehow, the conversation drifted toward my course in the United States. I told him about one of my friends from Fort Sill, who while in Afghanistan ordered his dog to be shipped to the country, but the poor animal never reached him.

The unnamed friend was rolling with laughter now.

"I know about your friend's dog."

I was curious, but he had to leave. So he promised to tell the story some other day.

Meanwhile, I pinged Kevin on Facebook that I had information about his dog.

The next week when I met my unnamed friend, I immediately asked him about the dog.

"That is one of the most interesting pieces of information I have ever had from my Taliban sources. You know that everything was very well settled on how to 'handle' NATO containers. There were charges for the driver, who would sneak out from the main route; for the guy who opened the lock; for the guy who re-sealed the container; and for the contractor who had pledged the 'safe' transport of the container despite the money that changed hands at the Afghan border.

"As luck would have it, someone paid for a container from which a dog of some rare breed escaped. The dog fled into the darkness of the bazaar when the door was opened. The driver and the man who had 'purchased' the container tried running after the dog, but jet lag and transatlantic travel filled the poor animal with such energy that it was almost impossible to catch up to the dog to find which way it had gone. Worried by the prospect of financial loss, the guy who had purchased the container tried to shift the blame onto the driver. But the driver was too clever for him. Returning half the money, he kept the other half. He then asked for a local dog to be captured, and locked him in the container. The purchaser of the container paid off the guy who had opened the container as well as the guy who re-sealed it. The driver then assured the purchaser that he would manage, and wished him the best of luck before resuming his journey.

"Upon reaching the Afghan border, the local dog – now caged for quite some time – instantly ran away as soon as the Afghan officials opened the container.

"A jirga was held and the damages were levied against the Afghan border authorities. It is said that the driver also paid some of the recovered money to the contractor who had first purchased the container and ended up having to lay out money to buy the decoy dog."

I could not bring myself to tell the story to my friend, who was once again waiting for his dog to emerge out of the porous Pak-Afghan border.

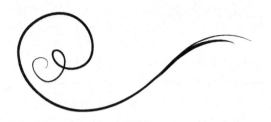

FOR LACK OF
SIGNAGE

STREETS AND TRAFFIC FLOW IN ISLAMABAD FLUC-
tuate almost organically, with ad hoc barricades and
security checkpoints part of the landscape. Added to
this, construction-debris spillover in the capital makes
driving according to the law anyone's guess. As a rule, if
the route was not blocked yesterday, it is likely to be open
to through traffic today. Yet precedent is no guarantee.
Predictability is the nemesis of all security protocols.

Among an infinite variety of routes I can take to
work, my favorite is a dirt-road extension that continues
off a perpendicular turn in the asphalt road, over a
rocky-pebbly slab of land where early in the morning
shepherds bring goats and livestock to sun themselves
and forage for food. For those of us whose vehicles graze
equally low to the ground, this sidetrack requires a slow-
down in speed.

If I am running late and a leisurely drive to work

is not possible, I may round the turn fully and proceed down the asphalt stretch past the sturdy edifices of Parliament House, the Prime Minister's Secretariat, and the Federal Shariat Court. This is the so-called Red Zone, a heavily guarded sector of Islamabad Capital Territory where security police keep a constant eye out for patterns and irregularities.

The tip-off to officials that I was either a foreigner or a neophyte of the city was my cruising speed in the wrong direction down Constitution Avenue, a central artery of the Red Zone. A security police officer waved me aside immediately. I removed my diplomatic plate from its intentionally hidden hold to display it prominently for identity purposes. He was disinterested. He pointed to the trajectory from whence I came and noted the long line of cars moving down the same road in the opposite direction. His lack of sympathy for violators of the law was evident.

I retraced my error mentally. The day before, I had used the same lane to travel south, and now suddenly it was open exclusively to northbound traffic. Less than a half-block down the road I could see the reconfigured cement roadblocks, forcing traffic into my lane in order to head north. The barriers of yesterday switched camps to become barriers of today.

Realizing how simple my miscalculation had been, I laughed. The officer did not appreciate my levity. He remained stern, awaiting signs of remorse. I waved my hands in all directions, as if to say: "Who could possibly tell from one day to the next which had become the politically correct lane to use?" But something got terribly lost in the translation, and he had no idea why I was flailing my arms around. I returned to basics in the English language.

"Where are there any signs on the road?" I asked futilely. "Where does it say that this has become a one-way street in the opposite direction?" My English was wasted on the security official. Not so my theatrics, which he seemed amused by, despite himself.

"Let's go to the police," he commanded.

"I don't think that's a good idea," I countered, with a smile.

I gestured to the dysfunctional traffic light ahead that was out, the security blocks and construction-site elements that had practically merged, and reiterated my flailing arm gestures intended to simulate the coming and going of traffic with no apparent order.

"Violation. Let's go to the police," he repeated, this time with his face very close to my window.

My smile widened. "Violation of what? There is nothing around to violate," I noted. "There are no arrows and no detour sign! How am I, as a driver, supposed to know what to do?" I was certain the specificity of my points were lost on him, so I further gesticulated to the unblinking traffic light for punctuation.

His stone face cracked a large smile as he realized he was operating in the midst of a traffic police wasteland.

That is how the morning found us – diplomat

and officer – returning each other's smiles, avoiding the police station, and sharing in the absurdity of the moment, all for lack of signage.

NINE PIECES
OF LUGGAGE

Jay,

Hi, from East Sussex.

It has been an eventful week. It did not occur to me what leaving the country was until I stood stranded at Heathrow with all nine pieces of luggage ... LOST.

I filled out the lost luggage claim form and, since I had to put in a mobile number for a mobile phone I had yet to buy, I provided the phone number of a friend who had moved here last year. Stupidly, I did not inform him that there would be a call from the lost luggage compartment.

Next, the taxi I had booked (for all that luggage and the family) left after waiting for three hours. I called the service again, and when I spotted the driver with the placard carrying my name, we instantly hopped in the car and exited from Heathrow. Before we could hit the highway, the driver received a call from his office: there were two Hassans at the airport, and he had picked the wrong one. Or to be precise, we had tapped the wrong driver.

When we reached our destination, it was raining heavily. Despite the fact that the driver was a Punjabi from the other side of the divide and that we had had a hearty discussion, he refused to wait for Amarah, who had gone to collect the apartment keys from the adjacent office block.

Finally, soaking wet, we ended up in our apartment, with no internet or telephone. Next morning I called the friend whose number I had entered on the form.

"You want to know about the latest scam?" he replied. "Someone from Etihad called me almost fifty times, saying that they had my nine pieces of luggage."

I patiently inquired: "What did you say?"

"I told them to F*&^ themselves, and that they could send it back to Pakistan."

Anyway, now I am in place. The kitchen is in working order and so is the TV and internet. I believe we have been able to get our act together.

I read your last piece and had thought of sharing my experience with you. I hope it will make it into our book.

Now that I am living in the historical town of Hastings, I shall have more time to work on the manuscript. You shall be receiving more pieces, more frequently.

Stay blessed,
Muhammad Hassan Miraj

DRY CLEAN ONLY

A PERIMETER OF OPEN STALLS SERVES AS A PRELUDE to dense traffic within Pettah Market, a neighborhood east of Fort, in Sri Lanka's capital city of Colombo. Unlike the bazaar's interior, which is segmented into specialized areas of wholesale and retail concentration, this outer row of stores lacks thematic order.

Dabbling in any market's exterior to strategically enter the interior is a fundamentally flawed approach, for part of the pleasure is surrendering to serendipity and disorientation. So I moved along the bordering streets asking shopkeepers for the perpendicular turnoff where I could leave behind the periphery and get lost in more intimate quarters.

"Small shops. Long shirts," I would say, pinching between thumb and forefinger a corner of my ankle-length Pakistani *kameez* (tunic), and slicing an imaginary cut-off point at thigh's height. I was in search of a Sri Lankan version that might spare me the twenty-four extra inches of cloth.

Humidity, market trash, and the sun's heat beat down on the asphalt as I picked through frocks and formless dresses that would make a mockery of my figure. Several shopkeepers directed me a couple of blocks down the main road for other options.

Five times I walked back and forth in the direction where the sellers pointed, but there were no tiny shops, women's clothing stores, or alleys leading to the bazaar's interior. Taxi drivers awaiting fresh clientele eyed my futile back-and-forth battle of the pavement.

I entered a large store and walked up four flights of stairs to the women's casualwear section. A department store experience was not what I had come all the way to Sri Lanka for, but five different shopkeepers in a language I did not understand seemed confident this block would put an end to my search.

Large sizes were small, and the small, minuscule. I began imagining myself in a flowerbed of color combinations I thought reserved for children's bed sheets. It no longer mattered what I wanted. What mattered was stock on hand and a Sri Lankan clothing solution to Sri Lankan weather.

The barefoot saleswoman was beside herself trying to land a sale. I was consuming too much of her time. The more she showed me, the less I found something I liked, though my resolve stiffened to make the cultural leap into this new color scheme.

With seven mid-length shirts draped over one arm, the saleswoman pattered toward the fitting cabinet. As she deposited all seven garments in my hand and was about to close the door, she whispered slowly, "c-a-m-e-r-a." I wondered if she was warning me against the temptation to steal or giving me a heads-up about voyeurism. Thinking about both, I moved in and out of the shirts quickly. Perhaps her intent was to fast-track my decision-making.

As I was about to pay for a shirt that burst into cascading orange-hued roses, I noticed the label said "Dry Clean Only" and pointed out this new wrinkle in the potential sale to the barefoot sales clerk, for I had explicitly asked for a cotton shirt that did not require dry cleaning. Desperate, she showed the label to her co-worker.

His English was more limited than hers, but his experience in sales, quite advanced. Without losing a second to the potential sale, he presented the solution. He formed a scissor out of his index and middle finger, and placed the "Dry Clean Only" label between the two scissor finger-blades.

"Cut!" he said.

CONVERSATIONS
IN TIME

"I THINK I WON'T BE ABLE TO EDIT THE PIECES while I am travelling," she said.

"I have a feeling that we will stay in touch. Even if you are not able to send me a long message, small snippets will do," I suggested.

"How about sending you Morse code? The pulsations will be a reminder not to stray or get lost. I learned it back when I was a kid," revealed Judith.

"But why?" I was curious to know.

"My father taught me to use Morse code, probably because we lived near the sea. Have you heard about the Navesink Twin Lights, in New Jersey? Some of the most amazing memories from my early days are from this place. Throughout my life, whenever I would go there it was to make important decisions, at the top of the hill looking out over the Atlantic, where Guglielmo Marconi's Morse code and telegraphic history is documented at the little museum on the lighthouse property. I had read somewhere that Marconi always wanted to learn about new things, dig deeper into the unknown world, and for that he would abandon the comforts of real life."

Judith's monologue ended abruptly and there was no chance of reconnecting due to our varying time zones and bandwidth issues.

Incidents from our childhood are like lighthouses. They emit beacons that resonate, pulse up and down, and continue to transmit a signal throughout our lives, reminding us not to stray from a given path. This is why the moment I most dread is when I am surrounded by a crowd. While I am at peace with the cavernous, whispering galleries of St. Peter's Basilica, exiting a metro is a nightmare. Tracing this psychological glitch back in time, I can only account for it with a memory from 1986. It was a wedding where I had accompanied my parents and my three-year-old sister. I was five then.

Upon entering the venue, my dad walked his way toward the gents, and my mom joined the ladies. Both believed that I was in the safe custody of the other parent. By the time, the bride was sent off amidst tears, prayers, and assurances by the groom to the bride's father, the sun was forty-five minutes from setting.

My father had to accompany the groom, and my mother had to fill in for a local version of a bride's maid. That was when both my parents saw each other and loudly confirmed, "Hassan is with you, right?"

Before an answer could come from the other side, they were darting from one end of the wedding hall to the other. It was 1986 in Punjab, Pakistan, and there was no concept of a rescue service.

What happened was I had ceased to be relevant as soon as my parents got bombarded with relatives and friends. That is when I started playing around. Chasing a cat, I ended up in a busy market. The hustle-bustle and my own loneliness took over. Scared and lost, I stood against a wall with a poster of my favorite ice cream as the only familiar object in the area. The wall was within a shop, owned by a veteran. The twentieth century was drawing to a close, but children were still a collective responsibility, and the old man had seen the war.

I cannot really recall, whether it was the weather, the January loneliness, or the approaching dusk's gloom that dusted off his memory, but he started talking about his life, his random youth in some unknown town, and people that appeared and disappeared in and out of his world. His prophetic words, however, are fixed in my memory.

"The more surrounded by people you are, the more of a loner you become."

Once it started to rain, I could see worries settling in his wrinkles.

"Your parents are such an irresponsible lot." He extended the tarpaulin to cover the empty Coca-Cola crates. All the other shops in the market had closed down.

That was when my father, scared and dishevelled, appeared on his Blue Honda A-80 motorbike and asked the shopkeeper if he had seen a kid. Before my father could provide the description, he spotted me.

The old man started shouting at my father.

"If you can't look after your son, better give him away to someone who cares." He then ordered him in.

"Get inside! Otherwise you will catch cold. It's January rain."

He gave my father a cup of tea from his thermos flask, and after a good long set of instructions, saw us off.

The old man and I became friends with the passage of time. I visited his shop regularly whenever I went toward that part of the city. The more I grew up, the more we talked about life, though he never stepped into his past again.

Eventually, I graduated and moved on, from local school to boarding school, to college and then Military Academy; from being single to married with two kids. My job and writing career also brought me some fame and a lot of admirers. The visits to town became less frequent, but I made it a point, whenever in town, to go and see the old man. I would tell him about my friends, social circle, and people around me, to which he would always respond:

"The more surrounded by people you are, the more of a loner you become."

Exiting the underground in London at Kings Cross, I realized it was so true. Out in the open space, as soon as my mobile phone received the signal, it started blinking a white light, an indication of incoming messages while

I was offline. In came the continuation of a message that Judith must have sent earlier.

"And the decisions that I made from this place changed everything. One such decision was to move to Japan and leave my long-time stomping ground and comfort zone of Latin America, a move that eventually led the way to Africa and, many years later, Pakistan … because I learned that the plunge into the further unknown opens the most pleasant doors of perception. Hope to catch up after two weeks."

EVERYTHING,
THEN NOTHING

Tiny, with tousled hair and clothing in tat-
ters, a boy with a rounded face approached the
driver's side of my car offering something I could not
make out in the dusk. I examined the little vendor
standing in the street. From a seated position, our height
was about equal. He made a pouting face and held his
palms flat against the side window to keep me from
moving further toward the red light. When his hands
slid, smudge marks and a film stained the window's base.

A gray and eerie sundown gave way to darkness, with
the rolled-up windows merely sealing in the surrounding
chill. The boy continued to stare into the car. His eyes
lingered on my hands as they gripped the steering wheel
nestled in hand-crocheted half gloves that left the fingertips exposed. The gloves were a sickly pinkish-beige
hue, a color that must have been amenable to the failing

eyesight of the ancient woman who fabricated them from her mountaintop village in Turkey.

With one fingerless glove resting on the steering wheel, I used the other to point to it. "The gloves?" I asked through a closed window that needed no un-mute button to be understood. The boy nodded his head in assent. He wore no coat or hat, and his hands were bare. I considered the outside temperature and his life among the streets in winter.

The light turned green. I accelerated slowly. Guilt bore its edges into the rest of the journey. I was off to complete payment for an item at a far-away store where the shopkeeper had agreed to await my return before closing for the day. When I arrived, the owner was out at a nearby mosque for Isha prayers. To idle away the time, I sauntered out of the store, circumnavigating the neighborhood's commercial center.

Pacing back and forth along peripheral sidewalks, I ruminated over my fingerless gloves and the gloveless boy. On the downside of a lopsided curb, three young men in a perfect triangle positioned themselves around me for business. In triplicate, each one thrust a foot-long rack of men's scarves toward me. The selection was decent and, no doubt, reasonably priced, but my urgent need was elsewhere. I was thinking about the boy, not these men, and encouraged the entrepreneurial group with a vague promise of "next time."

I turned off the side road, into the marketplace interior. Two light bulbs dangled from a string over a table stacked in woolens: hats, socks, scarves, gloves, leggings. I dug in. The vendor, trying to be helpful, brought to the surface from the disarray a variety of gloves in my size and in colors I abhor.

I stopped my search from beneath the piles and pointed with my right hand to the fingerless glove on my left hand, much as I had done in the darkness of the traffic light. "*Choti,*" I explained, holding an imaginary two-inch chunk of space between my thumb and index finger.

The guy knew his merchandise. He held out for my approval a small packet of yellow-and-pink-striped fingerless gloves. "A boy," I corrected, returning the packet to the fray but already pleased by his acumen. Fishing through assorted woolens, he produced a second tiny packet. It contained black-and-red-striped fingerless gloves. "*Bas,*" he said. That was it. End of selection.

I paid for and pocketed the Pakistani "boy color" gloves, fulfilled my before-prayer commitment much after prayers, and drove off determined to find the minuscule boy in the thickening darkness of traffic signals that all looked the same. It was now decidedly night.

Following the gently rolling hill lines, I decelerated at each traffic light. There were no human beings anywhere – little or full-grown. Three times I drove along the same road. At my third drive-by, I spotted possible movement in the shadows of the green divider. Thankful that it was a Sunday of reduced traffic, I slowed to a stop.

A diminutive figure was crouched in a crevice of the grassy divider. His back was to me.

"Hey!" I called out.

He turned and ran up to my window. The window was open enough to let in the crisp night air.

"These are for you," I said, handing him the packet of gloves through the window.

He stopped and stared at me. The two missing front teeth did not diminish the fullness of his smile.

"Thank you," he said, in measured but perfect English.

He skipped back to the safety of the divider.

The light turned green. I accelerated slowly, conscious of having addressed, full on, the issue of the moment, yet having done nothing for the larger needs of a life lived out among traffic dividers and the open-air chill of winter.

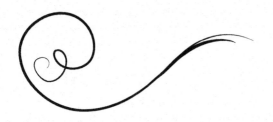

DAD DIARIES

"OK THEN. THAT'S IT. MAYBE," SAID MY FATHER in a matter-of-fact tone.

"Yes, that's it," I replied, though not in the same tone.

"Here is some money for the kids." He handed me a wad of one thousand rupee notes from his worn-out wallet.

It was the third week of December, and it had started getting reasonably cold in the evening. Abbu, my dad, had come to see us off. This was the second time I was leaving Pakistan for more than six months.

Last time, it was my trip to the USA, a promising point in my career. I had been selected amongst many officers and was the first in the family to travel to so-called wonderland, the United States, or what people back then referred to as "the States." It was 2009. Owing to the prestigious nature of the trip, he had come to see us off at that time in a much better emotional state. Religion had not yet defeated him in appearance and he had shaved, contrary to his present bearded look. Back then,

Abbu was in good spirits, as he knew I would come back. This, however, was not the case now.

Probably it was not only the matter of my return but a whole range of things. We (my wife and I) had been pursuing the plan to migrate for the last ten months. Keeping in mind the previous glitches at the last moment and wary of an unwanted barrage of questions, we did not tell anyone about our immigration plan. Only a week ahead of our flight did we reveal our intent to leave the country, for good. I would resign from the army – a dream job to which many looked in awe from almost all quarters of life – and would relinquish a very sociable lifestyle.

Other than that, it was the fact that I had made the decision on my own. I had not even consulted or discussed with him the biggest move of my life. This strong-headedness of mine reminded Abbu of his helplessness and how unbalanced life had become after the loss of his partner. Had my mother been alive, she would have reprimanded me for making such a decision on my own or, at least, shifted the blame onto my wife for having created the circumstances that made me want to leave. But why *was* I leaving? I had left this question to be answered in time.

Now that we were a day away from our flight, my father had travelled to Islamabad for the good-bye.

As a matter of ritual, he took out his wallet, removed some bills, and gave them to Fajr, my youngest daughter and his closest grandchild.

I was searching for ways and words to wrap up the

whole scene when Fajr called out: "Baba, look! Abbu is crying!" That's when he looked the other way.

After a few moments of awkward silence, he gave me a hurried hug and a voice came from a far-off distance.

"OK then. That's it. Maybe," said my father in a matter-of-fact tone.

"Yes, that's it," I replied, though not in the same tone.

After he had left, I sat alone on the lawn. The sun was setting in the background over sprawling Bahria Town when I realized that I had been sitting all by myself for almost an hour.

Amarah, my wife, walked over to me and asked: "Hey why are you so low?"

I smiled back and talked her out of the concern, but somewhere a thought crossed my mind. Most of the conversations I have had with Abbu were all about good-byes.

ROOM FULL OF
COGNATES

I MAKE MY WAY TOWARD THE MAN WHOSE MIND I know is never at rest. There are clumps of people to move through in the crowded home, and I am sidetracked by an introduction to a fellow guest whose name is so similar in its Italian and Spanish varieties that I am unclear as to which of the two languages we should continue our conversation in. Several sentences later, I catch a false cognate in his Spanish, and I conclude that Italian is his stronger suit.

Elsewhere, though I am not yet sure where, the delicate soul I seek lies within a massive maze of brain tissue, building a line of argument into every possible human interaction and cutting a conscious crescendo through flights of thought that remain out of grasp for most. His is a world in which logic and pleasure compete for performance space. Around him and me and a hair space between Spanish and Italian, light-hearted chatter in multiple languages fills the room with an indistinguishable hum.

Finally, the mind-forever-at-work is visible in a contiguous room, slunk into a portion of the couch, hips practically where others' knees would be, deep in conversation with his alter ego, a man of regiment and methodology, vigor and rigor. They make a stunning duo in the living room annex, jousting their way verbally through topics as disparate as history and fine wines.

The conversation meets no lull, only challenges in repartee as the topics weave in humor and more weighted contemplation. In a moment of tense consideration, the two minds reach a near aesthetic impasse over the intended meaning of a framed three-dimensional image on the wall containing an AK-47 swaddled in white gauze. The piece gives this common Pakistani assault rifle an air of the war-weary come home, an allusion to the wounded who can hope to heal only their external battle scars.

South Asian and European perspectives clash around the significance of the work of art, and whether to accord it such a status. The mind that never ceases asks whether the pristine weapon can be removed from its bloodied history. His gaze upon the frame becomes lost in a scene from the past, when the sight of blood seeping into the white snow of Azad Jammu and Kashmir, at the far end of a burning barrel, coincided with the extinguished life of a fellow countryman.

The man of regiment sees in the framed artwork a

tribute to an invention whose popularity has made it the number one weapon of choice throughout global conflict zones small and large, far afield of Pakistan and the rifle's origins in the Soviet Union. Neither critic poses the explicit question of why the hosts, in whose home we all find ourselves, were inspired to acquire the work and give it such prominence among mixed company in the living room annex.

As I watch the duet and duel of two speakers whose respective native languages borrow from entirely separate histories, real and imagined cognates interjected into the conversation take it to new heights of absurdity, transcending the need for concrete resolution on any single point of contention. Ambiguity engenders enrichment, though the great mind has not entirely shaken free the recollection of a Kashmiri death scene that still haunts him today. I sense him move out of the frame, onto the bloodied snow.

I think back to the blunt butt of an AK-47 against the bony mass of my own shoulder as I take aim at a bullet-ridden silhouetted figure, while hot cartridges fly around me in erratic directions. No mortality. No comparison. Within my frame, I have the luxury of firing at a target inert even before I pull the trigger.

ENTIRE OCEAN
IN A DROP [*]

SUFISM IS A CONNECTION THROUGH LOVE AND DEVOtion to truth, inner enlightenment, and God. Its able-tongued practitioners share their journey in verse and song, willing to accommodate even those for whom ultimate attainment may be out of reach. The music of Sufism has wide appeal, crisscrossing lines of class, generation, and political alliance.

Shirking fame, the superstars of the genre claim spiritual lineage dating back five to seven centuries. Families whose musical history carries forth the obligations of tradition embrace with the acceptance of fate the predetermined nature of their path. They – the heralds

---

[*]   "Entire Ocean in a Drop" was originally published in *Khabr o Nazar: U.S. Embassy Magazine News & Views,* in 2015. The title is from thirteenth-century Persian poet and Sufi mystic Jalal ad-Din Muhammad Rumi: "You are not a drop in the ocean. You are the entire ocean in a drop."

of destiny – are also the messengers of continuity with generations past. Over the years, extraordinary talent has emerged from the family folds, turning key figures into world legends.

I have cried during performances whose lyrical import I did not grasp and felt rapture by poetry set to music in a language I did not understand. By my own account alone, the mysticism in these haunting melodies is transferrable to audiences not actively seeking out the divine.

Sufi music can render a disparate crowd to conduct itself as equals among equals. "You are not a drop in the ocean. You are the entire ocean in a drop," said thirteenth-century Persian poet and Sufi mystic Jalal ad-Din Muhammad Rumi.

Musicians of Qawwali, or devotional ensembles, begin at a tender age. Their quest to master complex patterns of South Asian rhythmic structure is well served while they are still young. Their days pass in hours upon hours of observation and practice. Through recitation of verses in praise of the Prophet Muhammad and Sufi saints, their dedication to this chosen art form becomes sacred. This early childhood marriage pairs inheritance and willpower.

"The boys begin playing music before they are born," explains the manager of a renowned ten-person Qawwali group matter-of-factly.

During one Qawwali performance, an older woman made herself available to me among pillows and carpets and an audience sitting cross-legged in rapt attention.

Her eyes, framed in a headscarf of flowers the color of spring, caught mine as she took me under her tutelage.

"This song is all about God's love," the self-appointed mentor whispered in my ear, trying not to interfere with the quiet fixation that had descended upon the room but committed to making my experience with Qawwali a more informed one.

When a noticeable change in the tempo and rhythm of verses followed suit, my mentor felt obliged to explain the change in musical direction. The woman moved very close to my ear.

"This is love of a different category – worldly love," she told me, even more discreetly than before, unsure I was capable of distinguishing between the two.

In the dialogue of two beloveds, the singer's references incorporated innuendo and invocation to suggest a more tangible sort of love for which women of a certain age need not hide their appreciation.

For the self-effacing and noble-minded followers of the Sufi order, dichotomies cease to exist between yearning and longing as well as the spiritual and secular worlds. Coupled in endless harmony, Sufi music is like tying a turban. One never ties a turban the same way twice. Yet day in, day out, the wrapping continues.

Sufi begins where all religions end.

NOVEMBER BLUES

Hassan
Gaylord, Texas
4 Apr 2009
2216 Hrs

Dear Bilal and Baba,

Prayers.

These days, when human beings have won over reservations and raised massive structures in innocent woods, this landscape is an exception. Some hundred years ago, flocks of long-horned bulls grazed here, but these days they can only be spotted at two places – the real animals at Fort Worth's parade and the steel cast at Pioneer Park.

The lady assigned to the international students' delegation explained how at ranches and farmlands in the southwest, the cattle were branded for the purpose of identification and accounting. The Egyptians and other students from the Arab world, oblivious of their geographic legacy of Muhammad and Moses in which cattle grazing was associated with prophet-hood, listened with great attention. How soon men take to disconnecting from their roots and moving on.

Curiosity crafted an uncanny resemblance with the Kafkaesque Polish officer's face when he asked: "Why do they brand the cattle?"

"Since there are so many of them, the procedure is necessary to avoid any confusion," the informed liaison officer replied, and the sandy Rahim Yar Khan of May 2002 reeled into my memory.

Pakistan and India were locked, "eyeball to eyeball," as newspapers put the whole military escalation into phrase. Fresh from military academy, I was sent to the farthest post in the desert. A small thatched hut made of straw served as my room overlooking Derawar Fort, a sentinel that once stood along the magnificent and equally mythical river of Kakh.

One day, as I sat atop a lonely sand dune, I saw herds being swallowed in the silent folds of the Cholistan Desert, much like the caravans from Vedic times that appeared and disappeared in the Indus Valley. I had sent for one of the shepherds and, after a while, one of them stood by me in a care-free demeanour. He held the reins of one of the camels.

"What are these signs for?" I inquired about the strange signs on the animal's back.

"It is for the purpose of recognition and identity,

since there are too many herds coming to and from the pastures at the oases."

"How do you put these marks on?" I asked curiously again. The owner of the herd had chosen not to answer my trivial question.

"Our officer is asking how you emboss these signs," insisted the sergeant, elbowing the rancher into answering my question.

The cattle rancher started explaining how the iron was heated and a mark, which is the brand, is stamped on the back of a newborn calf.

A train of self-lamenting thought had already set in, steaming through my lieutenant's mind.

How can we excel? Probably this is the reason that our country lags behind. Nobody gives a damn about animal rights violations. How cruel of our countryside culture. Nobody would even think of anything like this in the "first world," as in Europe or the USA. This moment of self-admonishment was quite all-encompassing.

The liaison officer was not yet finished with the details of the branding procedure.

"These cowboys took special pride and creativity in developing their brands or signature. As soon as a calf was born, they would heat the branding iron and emboss it on the newborn calf. People in the historic district of Fort Worth still believe it to be an effective method for identification. In a little while, all of the international students will be taken to the museum where they can visit the display area and buy the branding equipment, if they want. People get their names or brands carved on these branding sticks, even if they don't have a ranch."

While the journey of exploring the outer world remains linear, the drive for the cultural world is circular for mankind, across the globe.

Prayers.

THE LAST
WORST TIME

A BLANKET OF DARKNESS SETTLED OVER THE COUNTRY, with its epicenter in Peshawar. That was Tuesday, December 16, 2014, a date no one will forget. Tomorrow marks one week from the horrendous attack on the city that conceived as its target school children under the age of twenty. Of the 144 dead to date, at least 132 were age nine to nineteen. Others in the hospital could succumb to their wounds in the coming days.

Before blowing themselves up, the seven attackers on Army Public School-Peshawar stormed their way through an auditorium, classrooms, and hallways, picking off kids with one bullet to the head and burning select faculty in front of their pupils. What happened was unthinkable, unspeakable – shame and evil and inhumanity compressed into an atrocity that parents throughout Pakistan, no matter how far from the center of sorrow, grieved as if the loss were their own.

On Tuesday, and for three days following, the country fell into a silence of respect for the little dead bodies that had become the nation's question to itself. How much had gone wrong for attackers to succeed in turning a place of learning into a bloodbath of tragic proportions?

Shops shuttered. Events were cancelled. People spoke in hushed tones. Meetings that were unavoidable began with a prayer for the dead. I have lost count of the amount of condolences I offered. Peshawar, the "city of flowers," had become more so, what with floral bouquets everywhere to the memory of the martyrs at the Army Public School and government-run Lady Reading Hospital.

Terrorist attacks have struck throughout Pakistan, but something was different this time. The deliberate mass targeting of innocent children hit a nerve, and people have had a visceral need to let the families of Peshawar know that the whole country stands with them. Every night civil society joins in collective mourning through candlelight vigils held not just in Peshawar but in towns and cities quite distant from the massacre.

A blood drive at the U.S. Embassy the day after the attack brought together the most diverse group of people, all of us responding to a sense of urgency for the wounded who we hoped could survive. Medical staff filled every available blood bag with the blood of over one hundred American and Pakistani donors who had waited in line solemnly to contribute.

Since last week, the government of Pakistan retracted

its distinction between "good" and "bad" Taliban, and the prime minister lifted the 2008 moratorium on capital punishment for terrorism-related cases. On social media thousands of people replaced their profile photos with solid black squares or with black ribbons of death. In the media today, I read that five hundred terrorists are to be executed in the weeks to follow. More blood.

At work since last week we have been busy undoing the many scheduled activities on our planned calendar of events through emails, text messages, and phone calls. Things have a way of changing quickly here, and the scramble to dismantle struck my Pakistani colleague as vaguely familiar. As he tried to put his finger on it, he asked aloud, but almost to himself: "When was the last worst time?"

We have lost count. Each time should be the last. But this time was the worst.

REMORSE

I CAN NEVER SEE KENSINGTON AS IT STANDS TODAY: a high street, a park, and a number of transport-for-London stops. For me, it will always have a first and foremost reference as the site where Rani Jindan was kept in her last days. Rani Jindan was the widow of the brave Maharaja of Punjab, Ranjit Singh, and a regent herself before the empire was colonized by the British. The only connection that remains nowadays between Punjab and Kensington, besides a few curry houses on High Street, is the collection of artifacts from all over Punjab at Victoria and Albert Museum, in the neighborhood.

My travel to Kensington, however, was not for the lesson in colonial history. A story had brought me there, the characters of which were awe-inspiringly free-spirited. It was about a Pakistani man, Dr. Shafqat Hussain, who was schooled in the U.S., married a half-American half-British woman, and spent his youth between the academic landscape of Yale University and the picturesque region of northern Pakistan. After so much back and forth, he now planned to return to Pakistan for six months, at a time when the immigration stream was flowing in the opposite direction.

I first came across Dr. Hussain as a wildlife activist who had enticed Yann Arthus-Bertrand, the famous aerial filmmaker, to film northern Pakistan. When Dr. Hussain started talking, he and I realized that we not only shared interests but also many friends. After the filming was over, he went back to the United States and I went back to my work, but his story had hooked my heart.

Many summers later, when Dr. Hussain visited London with his family, I thought it was a good time to see him and complete the story. They were staying at the apartment of Hussain's mother-in-law, in Hammersmith, near Kensington.

Two things had continuously distracted me in the apartment throughout his telling of the story: the presence of a large number of elephants in the form of murals, sculptures, motifs, wall hangings, tapestries, paintings; and a frequent chiming sound of bangles. The elephants came in every shape and size and had occupied almost all the walls, corners, window sheds, and bookshelves. The tinkling sound of bangles reminded me of small bells tied to the flowing curtains back in Punjab.

The wife of Dr. Hussain saw through my inquisitive glances and involved into the conversation her mother, who explained that her love for all the elephants and bangles dated back to her childhood. Ever since she read the story of *Babar the Elephant,* she started collecting elephants; and ever since her mother gave her a box of Indian glass bangles as a Christmas present, she was in love with this item of jewelry. Despite geographical displacement, both items qualified as universal symbols with deeper religious and cultural meanings.

Dr. Hussain's kids wanted to play outside, so all of us moved to the park along with the grandmother. My main character was busy teaching his young son how to bat, drawing parallels between baseball and cricket.

As the conversation drifted, the doctor's story intersected with his mother's. As an American who had moved to the UK after her marriage, the grandmother was happy that her daughter had settled at a place that was once her home. I asked her about significant moments in her life, and she chose to tell me one particular story.

"On the seventh of July, 2005, London saw four suicide bombings. Because the underground trains were hit very badly, commuters had to walk back from work. I was among those walking the route the tube could no longer travel. On my way home, I noticed a strange thing. Everyone I came across was shocked yet showed signs of resilience and gave a thumbs-up to other passersby. By nightfall, the media was reporting that the blasts had been carried out by four suicide bombers who had each worn a backpack to the blast site.

"The next day when I boarded the train for work, a young man moved into the train who wore a backpack and matched the ethnic background of the alleged perpetrators of the previous day's incident. He stood next to me, holding the yellow pole of the tube. It quickly crossed my mind that he might be another suicide bomber. At that moment, the young man turned back and looked into my eyes. It was as if he had read my suspicion.

"I got off after three stations, but for the remainder of time we travelled together, I could not look him in the eye.

"To this day, I regret that I did not tell him I was sorry. We should not let our fears dictate our life."

The son had finally learned how to bat. The family had to leave for a dinner, and I had to get to the tube station for my train to home … with a backpack.

CAPITAL CONTAINED

SOBERING EQUIPMENT THE AUTHORITIES ARE bringing in. The ride to work today was in silence, as I watched hundreds of young men setting out on foot and by motorbike to take on a day's labor that would require situational-specific equipment. Tightly clasped in a fistful or dangling off of handlebars, the riot gear marked the men in the dark blue uniforms who each carried a helmet, bulletproof shield, and crowd-control stick. They were bracing for an unusual day at work. Two political parties have scheduled a "long march" to eventually descend upon the capital city, where respective columns of supporters will converge along with two charismatic opposition leaders.

In Lahore and throughout Islamabad, particularly in the "Red Zone" where the diplomatic enclave and government buildings are located, a couple of thousand shipping containers have been strategically and increasingly positioned since last weekend so as to block entry and exit points in the two cities as well as to interrupt

the traffic flow for the throngs expected to join the protest rallies on major arteries.

A media report lodged complaints by the Pakistan
Ship's Agents Association for utilization of containers
that were stocked with goods ready for export and local
items destined for "up-country" suppliers. This may
explain the rise in food prices at the market this week,
though the direct connection to fuel shortages at the
pump is more tenuous. A colleague spent down on avail-
ability in the gas tank during her three-hour sojourn for
a filling station, only to be limited to the equivalent of a
five-dollar purchase when she finally found a gas pump
attendant ready to sell. The amount barely helped her
recuperate the resources consumed in travelling from
filling station to filling station, after which she settled in
at home with no gas reserve for future trips of either a
one-way or round-trip nature.

As with all challenging circumstances, the environment shone a lasting light on the individuals who carried
out distinct acts of courage. Among stories and flashbacks
in circulation, I learned of two young men on motorbikes
riding homeward through Islamabad on a similar occasion a couple of years back, when violent demonstrations
erupted over an Islamophobic film and a French magazine that published cartoon depictions of the Prophet.
The friends knew that the shift from difficult road block-
ages to impassible roadways could develop quickly, set
off by one unfortunate incident or an excess of caution.
Having survived the risks in traffic throughout the day

and judging the unrest to have died down, the two bikers decided it was safe enough to head home.

En route, a protest was simmering. From their simple uniforms, the mob judged the bikers to be policemen in civilian dress, and their egress was promptly blocked. Outrage and exhaustion did not stop one of the two from quick thinking. He began to bad-mouth the municipal police and indicated he himself intended to join the protest. Calling his bluff, the protesters insisted the biker curse out the police, for all to hear. It was the price they had set on his reaching the other side of the crowd.

"F**king police!" the motorcyclist shouted loudly to the angry crowd, to save his life and that of his friend. They had not worked extra hours on an extra sensitive day, only to lose out at this final stage of their hard-earned wages.

From the home front, backdrop to my confinement, I remained attentive to how the next few days might unfold. A couple of days prior, as opposition-government tensions were still mounting, I had posted on Facebook an ambiguous photo of a lounging cat seen through a padlocked gate painted in Pakistani-flag green. "Locked in or locked out. The keeper or the captive?" I asked, not considering my own personal parallel of the moment. A smart response came in within seconds: "That's what every Pakistani is asking about himself nowadays."

SOME ARE
BORN HOSTS

THE MORNING I SPENT LOOKING THROUGH OLD
photos in Rawalpindi tinged my search through
the past with sorrow for the present. Over two hundred
photos, covered in dust and cobwebs, had found their
resting spot slotted into seafaring trunks without any
apparent order of acquisition. The South Asian past of
this collection depicted Pakistan and India before either
came into independent being. It showed the faces and
feats of pre-Partition politics before the need arose to set
the one apart from the other.

The United States, too, was represented in the mix of
photos and personalities reaching across nations to create a
bridge of shared interest in the physical fitness of humanity.
In polo, wrestling, tennis, cricket, and other sports, the
captions described challenges that brought great pride to
sportsmen and their sponsors but also scored big for the
forging of bonds among peoples from distant lands. On

and off the field, private efforts to close the gap between nations inspire institutional reinforcement yet require constant care and feeding of the first order.

Save for the examples hung on the walls, the photo collection was largely hidden. In order to see what the full collection comprised, each photo had to be shimmied out of its slot from one of the trunks lining the perimeters of the two upstairs rooms, then raised above the trunk line just enough for the homeowner and host of the encounter to make a quick determination as to whether the visual content was pertinent to my specific needs.

The rooms were hot, and the homeowner was nearing the end of his patience. Too many photos to go through for a selection of so few that would fit my narrow specifications. He assigned his household helper to the task of dislodging the stubborn frames.

The elderly helper was of a large build and wore a solid-color off-beige cotton two-piece *shalwar kameez*. Although he was taller than the host, the perpetually bent head and slightly curved frame dissimulated the fact. He could have been the age of my grandfather, yet he was treated like a household boy wiping clean the neglect of time from aged photos, trying to predict every need of his master so that he could meet it, menially, to show his worth.

The homeowner concentrated on his search effort, trunk by trunk, with no break time. The helper remained with his back bent to pull up halfway each dirtied photo for inspection, give it a clean wipe, understand the gesture of rejection, shimmy it back down into the holding slats, and on to the next trunk.

The old man's movements weighed heavily on me. I could not pretend he was absent. His assistance was critical to our progress. Nor could I overly acknowledge his presence without irking an already irritated host. I kept my head cocked sideways to assist in the instantaneous assessment of each photo, but the limited portion visible was not conducive to making even an uneducated guess on my part. Only the host, who knew each photo intimately, could make that swift judgment call.

So I stood by, following the homeowner and helper along the perimeter walls, sweating generously due to the lack of circulating air, and contributing unilateral chatter to encourage the completion of a dirty and unpleasant joint effort.

When the task was over, I thanked both profusely. The unequal team had uncovered some historical gems that tied the United States to pre-nationhood Pakistan and to early moments of the country's history.

As I entered the car, the homeowner handed me a couple of hand-plucked flowers from his garden. It was a gesture of peace, and we both understood it so. Tension, though unspoken, had run high. Amazingly, he had not lost sight of our shared goal. We had wanted to depict our two countries in instances of friendship. But to get there, I had to drive him to decisions of instant triage as he plowed through the humongous obstacle of an un-archived collection. I drove him, and he drove his staff. The helper, an outside observer, paid an insider's price.

My wish for friendship extended to the here and now if the goal, like the frames, were not to be wedged in the grooves of time. In Urdu, they say, "some are born hosts, some are born guests." This is how I, a guest in the country of my host, ended up an unwilling partner in exposing the underbelly of subservience, all in an effort to eradicate it and prove the oneness of humanity.

CONVERSATION
WITH A TWO-TONED
ALSATIAN

"**S**IR, MAY I HAVE YOUR PERMISSION TO BEGIN?"
The General nodded in agreement. Calm prevailed, and amidst the glowing lights I started my show at the Command and Staff College, Quetta, the premier military training institute of the country with a century-old tradition of excellence.

I say "my show" because it was whispered by so many that this would be a make-or-break deal for me. Having declined on grounds of difference of opinion a previous appointment – a presentation slot given to officers for reviewing their command on professional knowledge and communication skills –, I noticed I was being written off by the system.

Attitudes changed, stories travelled (faster than I could imagine), and by the time I went on mid-term leave, half of the military knew of someone who had politely declined the offer of "constructive criticism" by the faculty. I had even made arrangements for an alternative job.

Confiding in my father how unhappy I felt during this course was more terrible than anything. Of late, he had started thinking about the stage he had set for his kids. One son in the military and another in the family business was an average Pakistani dream he had struggled hard to achieve. Before he could shake his head, denying me the permission to leave the military, the phone rang. I went to answer the call while my wife explained how I was suffering through a superficial life in Quetta. Colleges, I learned, had played my life, pole to pole. While Pakistan Air Force (PAF) College, my home from eighth to twelfth grade, had worked hard to get me out of format, Staff College was working equally hard to fit me back in, however limited its means may have been. By the call's end, Dad had agreed I should seek an early retirement. We waited for June, when the course would end. But that was not all, so there I stood again in the limelight.

"The aim of today's briefing is to coordinate the plans of our division," I began, until something happened that many at Staff College attribute to different terminologies. For me, it was just a slip-up, yet the instructors noted in their white note pads "STAGE FRIGHT." What followed in the next three minutes was the worst presentation I had ever made. Departing the stage, I even invited the wrong person up after me, and that probably drove the last nail into my military career. Nobody could laugh, as these sessions were religiously silent in nature, but I could see my colleagues beaming.

Staff College had cultivated a unique camaraderie in us. In the big room crammed with future leaders, I did not register a single worried face. They so thinly veiled their joy that even the reassuring looks I received told me how the audience actually felt. Back at my seat, I started analyzing what had happened and why. The 38 rehearsals I had carried out were immaculate. A public speaker since second grade, the stage rather comforted me, and having lived the life of Jekyll and Hyde for the past eight months should have easily gotten me through the three-minute act. Beside God's hand, which had intervened and hid the slides, I did not see any other reason for the episode.

Back at the session, while my colleagues apparently listened to other presenters, deep down they realized that I was no more the successful man they once thought I was – or could have been, had I presented well. They reached this conclusion so obviously that I did not have to wait for their comments. As for the elite group of learned faculty, they sent many looks of disgust my way. Nevertheless, toward the end, as part of an unwritten code of sportsmanship, everyone congratulated everyone for everything. Those who knew me commented on how I had spoiled the whole show. At this point, they thought I would be brave enough to take their honest comments.

I waited till the equipment was packed up and the audience gone, before walking sheepishly to my home.

Although it was quite late, I still could not avoid further comments.

"You did well," a course-mate greeted at the gate.

"It was not that bad!" an old class fellow consoled.

"Why did you ruin it?" my neighbor finally criticized. I had no answer.

Life, I had often vehemently explained to people, was beyond petty things, yet here at Staff College, I myself had fallen victim to it. The parables I wrote on autograph books while giving sessions to younger university students had lost their meanings, and "Smile no matter what happens" appeared to be such a farce.

Back home, the routine brooding of "no sweeper to clean the house," "last date to submit fee," and "absence of quality milk in the local dairy" awaited me. I tried telling my wife that I had had a bad day, but she did not know how to react. I took the kids out as a one-size-fits-all solution, but that, too, did not help. The city was off-limits, so we went to an on-campus coffee shop. The shop served as a reminder to students that at no time should they escape the habitat of Staff College.

At the counter, while receiving my change, I heard a voice, "Hey, what were you doing on stage anyway?" That was probably when I lost it. I came back, dropped the kids at home, and went for a walk. I passed by the Chief Instructor walking the grounds with his wife and his dog. This carefree stroll of half an hour towards the end of the career prompted many of us to trade our life's little happiness almost throughout the service. Roaming aimlessly on the dimly lit streets, I missed my usual care-free self, beyond the fear of being watched and judged.

The next day, things appeared less scary, but I could still hear folks behind my back: "He is the one who forgot the three slides." The instructor walked into the syndicate room and bombarded me with questions. "Why can't you simply read three slides?" "What is wrong with you?" "Didn't I tell you not to give up?" "Why do you always look confused?" "What is wrong with your thinking process?"

I stopped listening and smiled inwardly to myself. "Don't smile, it's not funny," I thought. "You were given a responsible assignment and you simply ruined it." I looked down, but then I heard the teachers at PAF College, who always taught me to look up in life, liter-ally and figuratively. I raised my head and looked up. Two friends sitting behind the instructor carried out their muted conversation by exchanging chits with notes written on them and giggling. It did not take an Einstein to know the content of the chits.

After class, I came back with a solution. My next-door neighbor had just bought a dog. I took the two-toned Alsatian and drove to a Hazara graveyard. The track to Koh-e-Murdar mountain range was winding but after three hours of trekking promised a rare scene: a decent and harmless view of Staff College. I sat there and started talking to the dog. I talked about how I felt when I missed the slides, when I realized I was speaking about one place and pointing at another, when I was called confused, and when someone disregarded my thinking process – a process I had worked so hard to develop. After I had emptied my heart, the sun set peacefully. It had waited to listen to me. I was lighter when I walked back, and felt relieved.

All it had taken was someone who could listen to what I wanted to say, to see how bruised I was, and to accept what I was thinking. At Command and Staff College, despite the vastness of its grounds and reach of its staff, I realized there was not a single living being within who was capable of being non-judgmental.

READING BELOW
THE POVERTY LINE

A S DISTINGUISHED MEMBERS OF PAKISTAN'S LITE-
rati filter into a room to take seats around a long
rectangular-shaped table at the center of an unadorned
space, students skirt their seniors to occupy additional
chairs placed, as a second tier, in an arc one row removed
from the center of power. The unclaimed seats at the
table are placeholders for elders still to arrive – legends
whose voices the youth have come to hear. At issue is
the culture of reading in Pakistan, and each stakeholder
present stands to lose a lifetime of meaning should the
written and recited word fall into disuse.

I am placed at the head table as chief guest, though
the late-breaking invitation that reached my inbox a few
hours earlier made no mention of the weight my presence would confer upon the solemnity of the occasion.
I am personally convoked, informed that I will share
in a movement whose purpose is to infuse youth with

the imperative of reading. Here, around the table, the country's literary elders need no reminder of the pre-eminence of their art form. Peers and participants treat them with unsolicited deference. With the arrival of each well-known figure, the pecking order shifts, filling in the peripheral circle of seating with the newly displaced.

In the yielding of chairs to spots of greater promi-nence at the table, the outer ring of seated youth begins to feel disengaged. They are pushed out of the center of literary gravity, and the message of the conference is thrown into reverse. A continuum of monologues over-takes the possibility of dialogue, leaving no room for the younger voices.

Eight preeminent Pakistani literati – poets, prophets of prose, playwrights – testify in favor of the cause being defended: the culture of reading and the value of books. Called to the witness stand are written works, whose texts the elders deliver with great eloquence of style. The room fills with sound, cadence, and emotion as the authors engage in constructive arguments and read aloud book-marked passages from timeworn editions of their work. For over an hour, the words pour forth in Urdu.

With the host to my right and a *grand dame* of let-ters to my left, we preside over this distinguished reading group making its way through entire segments I cannot understand. The youth ring is whittled to three.

The authors are on a roll. The week has been tough on them, as the trial of the former prime minister at the National Library in Islamabad turned their sanctuary into a courtroom. Eager to reconstitute themselves from such an affront, the group drives their words home and ceases to notice that the youth collective has now drawn down to a single individual. One author suggests that his peers contextualize their concern, asking how a child whose stomach is growling from hunger could care about reading.

Although I cannot understand any of the texts read aloud in the last hour, I do grasp much of the criticism and debate. The literary elders equate reading with books. Today's youth, who move in more interactive spaces, seek dialogue and devices, while youth lacking the luxury of three meals a day require none of the above.

It used to be that one who lent a book was a fool, but one who gave it back was doubly so. In this century, information-literate generations share and give back through commentary around the clock. This continuous sharing of views is hardly a fools' plate, and recent history has proven it can trigger meaningful global movements. In the virtual space, the outer ring freely rises to the center of power.

HIGH CONTRAST

A FEW HEADS IN SILHOUETTE IN THE FRONT ROW separated me from the panelists on the dais who were invited to talk about their enthusiasm for photography, its evolution as an art form, and basic principles of composition. "A love affair of life, for life," the moderator explained.

The speakers covered the genesis of photography and imparted to a youthful and largely uninitiated audience the trajectory of technology from an image that originally took eight hours to expose to one that a remote-powered robotic device, positioned hundreds of Earth days from the viewer, could capture through a transmission completed in seconds.

Each of the presenters had decades' worth of experience in their chosen profession of photography. The most senior speaker, a venerated member of Pakistan's inner circle of visual artists, was one of the last to present. Thin, calm, and elegantly elderly, his life's work was in calligraphy, painting, sculpture, photography, and – for a touch of incongruity – forensic sciences. The recipient of more than five hundred national and international awards spanning a productive lifetime, he was the organizers' choice to provide an overview of photographic composition.

Soft-spoken in nature, the microphone was of no interest to him. Thus, among the few who could follow his patient progression from Buddhist sculpture up through contemporary expression in the arts were those on his side of the room only: my row in addition to the first row in front and one behind. Beyond this limited quadrant, the sound system could barely project and it could not carry his voice to the twentieth row back, making the images on the big screen all the more significant as, for some, they constituted the only incoming information.

Although the exposé was in Urdu, the utilization of English for all technical terms made an otherwise unintelligible presentation quite transparent. The speaker moved from Buddhism through the centuries at a measured pace. Stop-off points included the Renaissance and the first photograph ever taken, by Niépce, from a window in France in 1826. After da Vinci's "Mona Lisa," he projected onto the screen Michelangelo's "Creation of Adam." The entirely unclothed figure of Adam with his exposed manliness illuminated the midpoint of the screen for a seeming eternity. God was absent from this closely cropped detail of the fresco, and Adam's private parts lingered in the center of our circumscribed universe for a tense four minutes that felt more like eight.

The nearly touching hands of Adam and God were the least of the crowd's focal points while the large hall filled with historical anatomy.

Time and space conspired to provide extended exposure to Adam in the nude. It was like Nicéphore Niépce's eight-hour composite through time-lapse photography, with the full length of the figure consumable at one sitting. The many teenage boys and girls present took keen notice of the unprecedented treat, as local schools typically shy away from anatomy in the classroom, let alone a zoom-in to such a publicly magnified degree.

Moving farther away from the microphone, the artist-turned-lecturer had no inkling of the adolescents' alternate appreciation of Michelangelo's work and continued to pontificate, quietly, losing himself in the balance of composition and light of the scandal-laden fresco and each of the images to follow. By the time he introduced the concept of perspective of depth, he was practically in rapture and had drifted so far from the microphone, that we, the audience, were left staring at the back of his head, while he succumbed to the works he advanced on the screen.

From the back of his head outward, libidos were abuzz and authorities seethed inwardly from the stinging moment when Adam had visited the room so unabashedly. Yet the senior photographer at the podium remained aloof. Art takes orders from no one.

The presenter moved on to the Rule of Third [sic]; to angles, texture, repetition; and to triangular, L, S, and diagonal compositions. Finally, the ladies in the room could exhale. And when he spoke of simplicity versus high contrast, I considered how he himself had demonstrated these concepts more than he realized. High contrast the images had been, indeed, but of a societal order.

BARBECUE CELL

MY FRIEND Z AND I SAT SHADING OURSELVES from the late summer sun while gazing upon the vertical puzzle that the Manhattan skyline forms along the Hudson River. From the Jersey City waterfront – over eighteen miles of pathway along the river – the view of New York City draws residents and tourists throughout the year. We were but a speck of two among an increasing crowd during the work-week lunch hour.

We talked. We gawked. We took photos along the railing that backed up against the water's edge and presented New York from a palpable distance. Nothing distinguished us from the diverse collection of people enjoying the intensity of the sun, as the end of September neared and each day moved closer to the onset of fall.

At Exchange Place, known also as "Wall Street West," we settled into serious conversation at a lookout point at the pier's end, beyond a memorial to restive souls who met their fate during the Katyn Forest massacre of 1940. We sat upon a communal bench made of wooden planks patterned in a geometric semi-circle open at one end to accommodate the comings and goings of visitors. The eaves above afforded protection from the sun.

The matter to be discussed was delicate and required my full attention. I watched Z steadily, alert for micro-expressions that would reveal the true wear-and-tear of his predicament. With my concentration on his face, I caught only part of what happened next, in an accident so freakish the before, during, and after of the incident merged into one.

Z may have been preparing to show me documentation on his mobile phone, or maybe he was sneaking a peek at the ever-active flow of information on the device. Either way, his original intentions were aborted. The phone, cradled for an instant in his hand, slipped directly from there into the slender opening between two wooden planks of the boardwalk-style communal seating area.

We looked at each other, amazed at such clumsy choreography and poor timing. Then we peered through the slat. The mobile phone lay inert in two parts. Through one slat its white body was visible face down among accumulated garbage. A few slats over, we spotted the silver case, which had separated upon impact.

Z paced the boardwalk and seating area for a crawl space from which he might retrieve the mobile phone, but the semi-circle was sealed shut. Not even a small child could enter the garbage-strewn area where the cell phone lay now in two pieces. Access would be a municipal *noblesse oblige* and a small miracle.

Walking swiftly, we caught up to a portly fellow in police uniform at the outer limit of Exchange Place. He agreed to accompany us back to the pier to examine the resting place of the mobile phone. There he confirmed on the spot the unlikelihood of anyone doing anything to assist. At any rate, his jurisdiction was limited to Port Authority. The boardwalk and planks fell under the authority of the municipality. He pointed us in the direction of City Hall, bidding us a friendly good-bye and good luck.

Z is an international student, having arrived in country only a week and a half prior to our meeting. He was in no mood or economic position to sacrifice his one lifeline to the homeland. We trod toward City Hall with the sun at its apex bearing down on our backs.

The woman at City Hall operating the metal detector suggested we begin our quest at the Resident Response Center (RRC), a "one-stop office for information or assistance related to City services." Aware that our request was not what a city of over 240,000 people might consider an emergency, I suggested Z highlight the international educational exchange nature of the case to drum up human interest and sympathy for something that was entirely his fault. I was also aware that the day's interactions with authorities would forever color his understanding of the relationship between civil society and government in the United States.

"I am an international student from Pakistan," he began, as he described events leading up to our visit to

City Hall and his loss of a connection, via mobile phone, to a land and people he loved.

"So, you see, it is actually an international cell phone incident," I summarized, smiling.

The two women were moved by the story, and it definitely punctuated their more run-of-the-mill complaints of the day. Z filled out a form to lodge an official complaint, and I proudly displayed to the women documented photos on my new Android of the boardwalk bolts, the slat through which the cell phone had passed, plus close-ups of the cell phone in two pieces among strewn litter.

"There is only one person who can get the job done," pronounced the RRC representative. "Carlos."

When Carlos and his son met us at the pier of Exchange Place about thirty minutes later, the crowd had thickened. From afar, I worried that the international incident had created a spectacle, but it turned out to be the popularity of a lunch spot with a view that made the pier a hot option where office workers could meet in the open air. A Mexican student spoke to his girlfriend via cell while sprawled on his back next to the planks that needed to be removed. I excused us for having to interrupt his intimate conversation and siesta.

Carlos got down on his knees. In seconds, he unscrewed two boardwalk planks with a power drill from his van of tools. With the planks removed, the two pieces of Z's cell phone were perfectly visible. Carlos then lay on his stomach and extended his arm toward the phone, but it was too far out of reach.

"*Sácame del van las pinzas ésas de barbecue*" [Get me the barbecue tongs out of the van], Carlos ordered his son in Spanglish. The son looked like he had put in his fair share of grill-side work and sprinted toward the van to get the "tool."

The barbecue tongs looked like huge steel lobster claws. They added a yard of reach into the bowels of the boardwalk. On this second try, Carlos removed the cell phone like a pro flipping meat on the grill. He deposited the two pieces of cell on the footboard, screwed the planks back into position with the power drill, rose to his feet, and dusted himself off. It was getting on time for a late lunch.

We thanked the father-and-son team profusely, particularly for their innovative end game. Z had been lucky that no water lapped beneath this part of the boardwalk. He was even luckier that a man named Carlos, fond of grilled meats, stashed a pair of barbecue tongs among essential tools in the emergency response van of Jersey City.

PAKISTAN, YOU HAVE A MEDICAL SCHOOL THERE?

IT HAD TAKEN A LONG TIME TO LAND AT DALLAS FORT Worth. Finally, I could now tell my folks that I was in USA. The military training, scheduled to start in November, had been called off just a week ahead of the travel dates. As I returned from the U.S. Embassy, I broke the news to three-year-old Fatima.

"We won't be flying to USA this month."

"So I will have to put up with my teacher for how long?" she asked.

"Ideally, two more months, or maybe longer," I replied, keeping in mind the uncertainty factor that plays at large when military training abroad is involved.

Three months later, when I had almost given up and was sitting on the mess lawn, I received the call from the U.S. Embassy. We kept on confirming to ourselves that we wouldn't really be flying until we took off for Abu Dhabi, a transit point for Houston.

After the initial weeks, we concluded that people in the sleepy town of Lawton, Oklahoma, knew as much about Pakistan as we knew about the rituals of Comanche burial.

Their knowledge about us was largely confined to the hawkish media reports and the stories from veterans deployed in Afghan cities bordering Pakistan. Initially, I tried my best to clear the air, but then I decided to act otherwise.

We were housed in an apartment block adjacent to the training facility, and soon life took its form. My wife, Amarah, joined the Red Cross service in the neighboring medical facility, and her benefits won Fatima a place in the day care center next to the hospital. We could only realize the influence when she started speaking Spanish more fluently than her mother-tongue Urdu.

There was little to be learned from the military training, as it was a refresher of all that I had studied back home. Every evening, Amarah, Fatima, and I would go to the nearby park and spend some time there. Fatima was the first to strike a conversation with the kids playing, followed by a pickup in conversation among the women and, lastly, men shook hands. Somehow, Oklahoma reminded me of some liberal parts of my own country. People often asked questions about Pakistan, but nothing struck us more than a conversation with a veteran Marine.

It was our third month in Lawton. The pattern was pretty much developed. All the playground acquaintances in the park were now good friends and were already hooked on Pakistani food. One evening, as we were sitting in the park and Fatima was playing with a lone kid, we saw an old man approaching the play area.

As he was close enough, Fatima's playmate ran toward the man and pulled him along to introduce Fatima.

The old man talked to Fatima, while we closed in.

He extended his strong hand.

"Sergeant Grey, U.S. Marine Corps."

I introduced myself, and then the routine conversation about the military and the country started. He then asked about Amarah. On hearing that she was a doctor, a visible surprise lit up his plain countenance.

"Doctor?" he asked again.

"Yes. In fact, I am training to be a specialist in diagnostic radiology," Amarah replied.

"But how come? Did you go to India?" he asked.

"India? Why would we?" It was our turn to be surprised.

"But ... wait. Do you have medical schools there in Pakistan?" His question was only answered by our laughter.

Next Sunday, when he ate with us, I invited Dr. Fouzia and her family to join. Hers was one of three Pakistani families in that town. Mike remained surprised when he was told that Pakistan had the world's seventh largest pool of doctors and engineers. On the other hand, he was sad to learn about the dilemma of

South Asian parents, who could either live with their grown children or resign themselves to watch them succeed and move out.

AMERICA.
BAD COUNTRY,
GOOD COUNTRY

T HE TWO BROTHERS NEVER REST. THE YOUNGER ONE sleeps at the shop, literally. The weave of business relations and personal ties are such that favors are a mainstay, despite theoretical working hours. "Always work, never rest. Whenever you come, we'll be here," was the younger brother's categorization of the store hours when I attempted greater specificity.

The outfit caters to changers, receivers, and senders of money. Aging, oversized reproductions of the many notes of legal tender in which the store deals grace the walls in a lackluster decor drawn exclusively from a currency motif. Whatever the season, it remains gray indoors. Outside, a guard with an AK-47 consumes half of his job in inattention. I view him as well as the street through the back part of the head of Benjamin Franklin, on a two-feet-long decal of a U.S. one-hundred-dollar bill. As I wait to complete my transaction, I feel as if I am looking out onto the world from the inside of a bill.

"Passport," the young, surly brother demands.

"America. Bad country," he pronounces unflinching, as he receives it.

"Why do you call it a bad country?" I probe, not knowing if that line of inquiry is a good idea. His strong emotion comes from somewhere, and I want to find its source. I cannot restrain myself.

"No visa," he answers.

I ask him why he would bother to visit a country he does not like, which further pushes my finger into the wound and moves us a step closer to the relevant information held back.

"My brother. The United States."

Uncertain about whether to add a preposition, I ask if the brother is living in the United States. Smirking, I also suggest that the brother may have a different opinion about my country, given his present location.

Just then, the cell phone rings. The older brother in the United States is calling to check in on things with the two brothers in Islamabad. His morning is our night. Lots of smiling and speaking in Urdu follows. The fact that I am waiting to finish my transaction seems totally irrelevant.

I mouth with my lips, "brother in America?"

He nods smiling, continuing his conversation with the person who lives in the country he hates.

He eventually hangs up, and our transaction resumes. My passport is returned, and no further

158

mention of it is made. We enter neutral territory; the family as mollifier.

Nothing about my transaction resembles a round number. I hand over the payment I prepared in advance in order to save time. All of my money is pre-counted and separated into individually labeled packets that facilitate counting and verification.

The younger brother is visibly moved. He is beaming. Maybe I am the first ever to render his calculations an easy task. He completes the tally in 10 seconds.

"United States. Good country." His revised conclusion appears to be based on this newest set of observations. But I know what he means. Time is money. The same Benjamin Franklin stuck on the window said so in his 1748 *Advice to a Young Tradesman*. In this money shop in Islamabad, more than two and a half centuries later, even the reverse is true.

RULE OF THIRDS
THROUGH A
GRATED WINDOW

T HE WROUGHT IRON CROSS BARS THAT INTERSECT my top-story window view of the Margalla Hills offer a resting spot for a small green gecko lizard and, when it slithers away, for a tiny bird that hops from bar to bar. Signs of life and nature outside stand in contrast to the lack of movement within, on my side of the metal bars, as I wait out the critical days of the solemn month of Muharram, the first month on the Islamic calendar and one of four sacred months in Islam. Today, the tenth day, is what various sources call the "climax of the mourning."

Already yesterday, for the ninth day, federal authorities ramped up vigilance with helicopters circling overhead in Islamabad to better monitor processions from on high. Provincial and federal authorities, with military and paramilitary in tow, joined forces to control cities that can gather mourning crowds in the hundreds of thousands. The government deployment includes over five thousand personnel from police and law-enforcement agencies, dogs, surveillance cameras, and plainclothes agents. Robust security plans encompass as well the suspension of cell phone service for up to twelve hours a day in almost all of the major cities and in so-called sensitive towns.

According to newspaper reports, State security forces detained "an alleged Afghan agent ... wearing a jacket stuffed with about five kilograms of explosives" in Islamabad yesterday. The man was purportedly planning to attack a procession in the city the same day. In the capital of Pakistan-administered Kashmir, a cleaning crew along a procession route uncovered another ten kilograms of explosives in an improvised explosive device hidden within a heap of gravel.

Still, despite headlines on the order of "Efforts to snatch peace from the jaws of threats," the processions have been able to mobilize the masses in relative peace though, in keeping with the ritual, some participants do perform self-flagellation to their chests or, with blade-tipped chains, to their backs.

This year, Muharram is peppered by the added tensions of recent strikes against the Taliban, including the supposed assassination less than a handful of days ago of a senior Haqqani militant network fundraiser on the outskirts of the capital.

Given the very tangible threat perception, my to-and-from work movements are currently confined to zero. The single roof of my home is the exclusive reference point for the present. Beyond that, I cannot venture. At night, I hear fiery voices ring out from not-so-distant mosques, scratchy voices whose content I cannot understand but whose passion I can.

I read. I write. I work the e-mail circuit for developments related to my desk job. I move from downstairs to upstairs and, during daylight hours, on and off the balcony terrace for outside air and sunshine. On the Pakistan government-run radio station, round-the-clock plaintive chants remind one that the mood is somber, and indeed, it is.

THE AWARD

"**W**HO IS THE PATIENT AMONG YOU?"
The oncologist threw a hasty glance and the patient, my mother, was overjoyed. My parents and I had waited for two hours before being ushered into the oncologist's room. I replied to the doctor, but soon the questions were directed toward my mother, who was still joyful for the doctor's compliments on her health, not realizing that it was his usual trick to pull his patients up from the deep dark pit called cancer.

October 8, 2005, was not just the day that put Pakistan on the humanitarian aid map for a massive earthquake, but it also shook our lives. What appeared to be a lesion on my mother's lower jaw turned out to be a *Poorly Differentiated Squamous Cell Carcinoma* in pathological findings. My father did not understand these words when he received the report. On his way back from the hospital, he stopped for his usual mile of evening walk, and that was where the prescription slipped from his pocket, only to be picked up by his friend, a radiologist by profession. It was he who broke the devastating news. No one from our family had ever had this disease, so the mere diagnosis was traumatic.

As the nation reeled from aid and an unprecedented humanitarian experience, my mother underwent surgery after surgery. A month later, when Chinooks became a familiar sight in Pakistani skies, she was back to her normal routine.

She planned the fresh décor of our new home, acquired after pursuing my self-made father for almost 26 years. Having withstood her suffering long enough, living that quarter of a century in a small house with my paternal family, the only silver lining was convincing my father for this new house.

I now believe that my mother's comeback was largely motivated by her desire to give the house its final touches. She had done it so well that anyone who visited us in those days always left with praises, although carcinoma is not known for valuing all those admirations. The cancer, which was scrubbed off by six doctors in an operation stretching for eight hours, recurred within eight months. Before we could decide on the treatment, it had quietly moved through her veins and metastasized.

I was the first one, amongst my siblings, to know that she would not make it. I made use of my hard-core training and distantly saw her slipping away, while my family hoped against hope, day in and day out. She passed away the next August. I wrote the text of her tombstone, which summarized her struggle for a house of her own.

From One House to Another
Rubina Shaheen
Dec 1958 - Aug 2006

I did not shed a tear when I hugged all my siblings to console them, not when I lowered her into grave, not the following month when we gave her effects away for charity. It came years later. I had won an award in Rome, and I picked up the phone to share the news with someone I thought would be the happiest to hear the news. It was then, right there, at the Air Force Museum next to calm and peaceful Lake Bracciano, dressed up in my military ceremonials, that I realized what mothers meant.

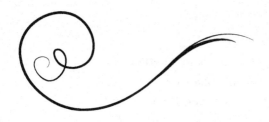

PULL OF THE TIDES

Until I could process my mother's passing, it was unlikely the ink would separate from the tears.

IT WAS MY MOTHER'S WISH TO GO QUIETLY AND WITH dignity, a lucid plea made to my sister and me with the little strength she could muster, as she faded into that place we dare not venture.

The death of my mother brought on a memory swipe that would wash over me in waves, moving backwards and forwards, confusing past and present, touching a space within me where she would eventually settle. Sometimes I would forget to remember, catching myself in half-thought-out gestures, futile missteps of time and actual circumstance. Like when I began selecting for her a brightly colored handmade oven mitt as a gift from Haiti though she was no more of this Earth to receive it.

When the tears swell, I look upward to wish them away and to control the flow, reminding myself in a soft, low voice that death is the irreversible lining of life. Then I summon the scene of our penultimate encounter, when my mother receded on and off into a state of uncontrollable exhaustion, asking rhetorically why she could not keep awake in midday, amidst the courtyard sun. Always, after this scene, comes the final one: a frozen expression never to be renewed. Back and forth the memory comes and goes, like a tide in motion responding to larger forces at play.

The curtains close around my mother's corpse. Three attendants prepare her body before the final pull of tides out to sea. They and I are the only witnesses to this most private moment. In respectful silence they toil, conscious of being the first in the line of protectors on my mother's one-way journey.

In the weeks following my mother's move to the afterworld, I rummaged through her belongings in search of a keepsake to honor our relationship. The direct contact with the minutia of her everyday life felt intimate yet raw. In a shoebox on a high shelf, I shuffled through all variety of printed greeting cards from the family, particularly the grandchildren, to wish her well on various occasions. I assumed the contents were dedicated to grandmotherly treasures and put the container back among some fifty other shoeboxes, distracted by the overwhelming number of details breathing belated life into death.

When a small packing box reached my doorstep a couple of weeks later, I was not entirely prepared. A large manila envelope rested atop an assortment of kitchen items and part of my mother's global teacup collection. Within the packet were dozens of handwritten letters I had sent to her over the decades from near and distant lands that I had called home, including France, Argentina, Burkina Faso, Japan, and Mexico. These vital accounts document emotions and events off my personal timeline that I had forgotten. As October and November had been a blur, the clarity of these written accounts caught me off guard. The discovery of the cache of letters led to another discovery: through the written word, my mother and I shared a connection I had no idea she valued.

In an envelope made flashy with a patchwork of commemorative stamps, I found parting words sent before I moved to Buenos Aires with a tiny suitcase in hand and a typewriter for what turned out to be a five-year hiatus from the United States: "Despite the limited on-board baggage, my heart is travelling southward, filled beyond capacity with appreciation for having a family that believes in love and the pursuit of a dream."

To be on this side of history, reliving moments of my own personal evolution over time in words destined for someone else's eyes is a gift of mirrors and mortality that neither my mother nor I could have intentionally constructed. Indeed, though she is no more, there is a place within me where she dwells.

INTERFAITH TUK-TUK

J AIPUR LITERATURE FESTIVAL DREW OVER FOUR HUN-
dred speakers in 2015 for discussions on literature
and contemporary politics within its tented fora, in
Rajasthan's capital. Intellectuals flock to this city from
across India and abroad, creating a crossroads for the
passion of words and ideas. During the five-day intel-
lectual junket, festival-goers contribute to the local
economy, as they take in the rich cultural heritage of
India's desert western state.

In winter, Jaipur is brisk and cold. On the second
day of the festival, organizers suffered a mixed blessing
of rain, turning unpaved pathways into pools of soaked
earth and prompting massive shifts in scheduling to
compensate for the open-air flooding. The temperature
dropped further at night, dashing participants' hope
for a modicum of warmth following a full day of bone-
chilling rain.

Evening musical events required a six-mile jaunt
over to a hotel far from the main festival venue. The cab

fare to and from the venue was higher than the norm, and the risk that transport options might be limited on the ride back, due to the hour and isolated location, was real. Maybe the arrangement was a way to win favor with the transportation union, to assure they had their cut of the festivities. My best bet was to invest in trustworthy private transport for the evening.

I searched my bag for a mobile phone number I had scribbled on a scrap of paper the night before and composed a text message to the young tuk-tuk driver who had proven to be impeccably honest in getting me from the train station to my hotel, following a five-hour Delhi-to-Jaipur train ride and nighttime arrival in the provincial city.

The station had been thin on women and thinner on security, and my unusual presence was gathering more attention than suited my comfort level. I arrived into the already darkened hours of the evening. The threat of harassment in the desolate parking lot of the Jaipur train station was palpable.

When I slipped into this driver's tuk-tuk, I looked the driver straight in the eyes. I needed to gauge his honesty, and that exchange was all the reference points I had at my disposal. He sensed my challenge, and handed me back the prepaid tuk-tuk fee.

"We arrive, you pay," he said in telegraphic English, setting me immediately at ease and demonstrating that, despite his age, he was a veteran at navigating the world of strangers arriving in his magical land.

We had a decent cultural exchange during the ten-minute ride to my hotel.

"I'm a Jaipur boy," he explained by way of street credentials.

"Everything is possible in India," he stated.

"There is only one thing not possible. Do you know what"?

"Nothing!" he answered before I could guess, smiling with a sideways turn to me, as I sat on the raised board in the back.

He specialized in off-alley short-cuts, affording me an evening view of the inner matrix of the city. This scored him further cultural points. He had neither rear-view nor side-view mirrors. On the main road, he was all intuition. He dodged horns and screeching brakes, weaving in and out of bicycles, man-powered rickshaws, motorized tuk-tuks, low-set sedans, and SUVs.

"Why don't you have any rear-view mirrors?" I asked.

"They distract me."

When he pulled up to the curb alongside the hotel, I added a fifty-rupee tip, instructing him to buy a rearview mirror so he could live to see the many years that lay ahead of him or, at least, tomorrow.

"How did you know?" he asked.

I did not understand if he wondered how I knew that he was driving without a rearview mirror or that fifty rupees would cover the cost of an inexpensive car part to remedy the situation. Not wanting to go into the minutia of fine English, I said, "I just know."

Like any tuk-tuk driver working the tourist influx to the city during the literature festival, he slipped me his number before I alighted, assuring me: "If you ever need a tuk-tuk …."

So when it came time to choosing between hailing an unknown tuk-tuk driver at night on a busy thoroughfare or helping to support an honest young man earn a living, I sent a morning text message to the "Jaipur boy," asking if a round-trip fare to and from the musical venue would be possible that night. I knew that my ride would be without rearview mirrors or frills and entirely ventilated with open-air chill, but the guy behind the motor-powered handlebars was someone who had earned my trust. In addition to honesty, he possessed all three items indispensable to maneuverability within India's major cities: a horn, solid brakes, and guts.

The young rickshaw driver arrived at the accorded time and braved mind-boggling traffic to take me to the performance grounds outside the city center. We bonded over traffic jams. When he learned I lived in Pakistan, he told me his real name. Unlike the adolescent nickname he shared with me the evening before, it was a classic Islamic name born of tradition and history. Under the prevailing pro-Hindu platform in the country, he embraced his Muslim identity with some degree of uncertainty and trepidation, though his wish was simply for interfaith coexistence. He confessed to a long-standing curiosity about Pakistan and indicated he hoped to visit the neighboring country some day soon. His kindness inspired me to offer a ticket to enter Pakistan thru its music that evening, as Sufi musician Sain Zahoor was the featured performer at my intended destination.

Uncertain that I meant business, my driver-friend lingered far from me at the ticket counter until, victorious, I flashed the purchased ticket. During the performance, we sat in the center aisle, a few rows back from the stage. I wanted to make sure he got a good look at Pakistan.

Sain Zahoor, the "roving minstrel," shook his single-stringed *iktara* and spun in circles. The young tuk-tuk driver understood enough of the lyrics in Punjabi to point out to me that one of the songs professed the need for Muslims and other faiths to live together, vindicating his earlier point about interfaith harmony in the middle of the cacophony of horn blowing and tire screeching. He was radiant. I turned to him from well within Indian borders and said, "welcome to Pakistan."

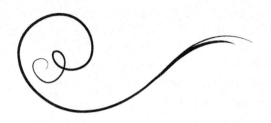

MOON
SPLENDOR RESET

S AND MOVES THROUGH THE HOURGLASS, A PROGRES-
sion having the upper hand in determining my
imminent future. Days earlier, a curtain of rain washed
over the nearby hills to the north and pounded the surface below, making it seem as if the inevitable could be
altered. Maybe Pakistan would not recede gradually into
the well of memory but could remain at the forefront.

The moon last night dispelled such notions. Full and
fleshy, its splendid illumination reset expectations, making
it clear that my environment would soon acquire new
texture. Honored, touched, and forever changed, I leave
Pakistan with a great feeling of loss. Yet through the experience itself and the people I have met, incalculable gain.

"I keep it as a symbol of you with me" (*app ki
nishani meray paas rahay gi*), a friend said of my parting
gift to him that barely touched the surface of how the
friendship formed or why it resonated so. Pakistan has

been generous, offering a multitude of gestures I now take with me as a two-year composite.

The life of a diplomat is itinerant, with the wish to stay endlessly coupled with the imperative to depart. Everywhere there is strength and beauty, struggle and challenge. It is up to the individual to stake out turf along that continuum.

A LETTER FROM
SIACHEN [*]

Dear Amarah,

"We, the willing, are doing the impossible for the ungrateful. We have done so much, with so little, for so long, we are now qualified to do anything, with nothing."

This quotation was written diagonally on the first page of his diary as he showed me his poems. My host is a young man, whose spirits are still volatile despite the sub-zero temperature of this place. It is our first meeting. He does not know that the quotation is by Mother Teresa, he does not know Mother Teresa at all. He thinks it was said for him, dismissing any reason for researching its origins. The young man got engaged recently, the reason for an occasional blush whenever the subject of his future comes up. I only reached here

---

[*] "A Letter from Siachen" was originally published in *Dawn* (2012, republished 2016).

the night before, but we are close friends now. There is something in the wind, with flakes, that urges people to speak in never-ending monologues. Discuss emotions, exchange secrets, talk about themselves – things they do not talk about "normally," not the least when they are engrossed in the workings of the "civilized world." I asked him about the quotation on the wall and he said let's call it a day.

My room, call it my studio apartment, is a typical bunker, built on self-help basis, thanks to our meager resources. Carved out from a hillock, it is a classical one-window room of 14x10 feet. The 10-foot-high ceiling has 70 girders. Trivial information, you say? I count them every night before I can sleep. No, I have not grown insomniac, but I dare not venture out to count stars in this part of the world.

On one side, the empty cartons have been arranged, covered by gunny bags, only to be topped by the prayer mat. I have a lot of time to pray and reflect, probably since I am the closest I could get to Him. The other wall supports the bed (an arrangement of empty cartons) upon which lies an air mattress, along with our sleeping bags. Tastefully, the big-flower-print bed sheet does not permit the attention to drift to the poor structure of the bed. The dark toilet is an extension of the same room. An old cough syrup bottle has been modified with kerosene oil to serve the purpose of the lamp which practically lights up nothing. The empty ghee cans are our make-shift geysers. Basic instinct is the best aide when it comes to anatomy in the dark bathroom. The room décor is an artistic arrangement of the empty containers of food, fuel, and fire. Food cartons serve as tables, fuel cans as stools, and empty (fired) cartridges as bedside teapoy items. The most decorated table has boxes of chicken cubes, noodles, egg biscuits, brick-game and yes, our window to the world, the radio. Other inhabitants include a Fujika (a kerosene-lit heater), petromax, the books that you have sent, and the military phone – this masterpiece of technology which connects me to you, remains silent. The weather, the snow, the wind, the electric power – everything conspires against our probable communication. Reminds me how Shah Latif narrates the plight of Sassi after she had been robbed of Pannu:

> "The camel (which carries Pannu) is my
> enemy, the wind (which is erasing the foot-
> prints of caravan) is my enemy, the sand is
> my enemy and so are the brothers of Pannu.
> And most of all the sun is my enemy, for
> having risen so late and not waking me up."

Our high point of the day arrives when we sit down for dinner. Fresh vegetables are a luxury. We live on roasted onions and tomato puree, which is canned. The weather denies us the luxury of fruit and vegetables, and much more. After getting over with dinner, we gather around the radio and switch it on. This really is the world on our fingertips. There is no FM here, only the BBC and loads of incomprehensible regional channels.

The alternative to BBC is Radio Pakistan, which runs the night-time transmission. About the night-time transmission, it is the radio's revenge from the television for morning shows.

Another day has gone. The vigilant sentries change over their duties. Far from home, away from gatherings, phone calls, SMSs, these men, I think, are doing something which can never be monetized. Purposelessly, looking against the ravishing snowstorms, their biggest foe is the weather. You can never predict its move. It sulks within, and you only realize how loosely you hang between a life and death when it hits you. A minor headache turns into cerebral edema and a man full of stories, intentions, commitments, and emotions becomes what they call a "casualty."

The radio is tuned up and we start receiving our dose of military bashing. A whole lot of qualified individuals start describing us as a merry-making mob, with no clue about how one can party at 20,000 feet above the mean sea level. My mind races. Huge chunks of budget for tomato puree and canned vegetables. Power hungry for morally supporting everyone that we have, people who love us and people who are the reason we live to guard this piece of land. Luxurious lives in a make-shift room with empty cartons. I think the quotation on the wall is not so over-rated.

Hope to hear from you soon...

Yours faithfully,
Hassan

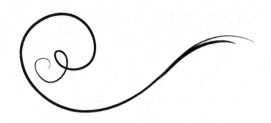

OPEN LETTER TO A
PAKISTANI PUBLIC

March 9, 2015

Dear Reader, Whom I Have Yet to Know,

As with all letters ever written, I reach out not knowing when and where you will begin to read these lines or under what circumstances my world and yours will intersect. The imperfect strokes of my handwriting cross continents and bridge a thousand possibilities of distance, focusing our one-on-one conversation to the process of your undivided attention. My letter to you opens up an exchange of views and ways, dreams and communities. In this back and forth of handwritten missives, we learn how the environment may nurture some and test the resilience of others. In the lost art of letters, regained through "Handwritten with Love," no character count or immediacy of purpose holds us to the task. No text is remotely predictive. Letters re-establish a connection of ideas and emotions that transcend time and space.

From the United States to Pakistan, handwritten with love, Judith Ravin | Cultural Attaché | U.S. Embassy-Islamabad

I imagine your faces in advance of seeing who you are. An audience as yet undefined.

As I grapple in my mind for a connection that will draw you near, I realize that you and I are merely two sides of an ink trail. The YOU I cannot see, and the ME you do not know. A possibility for dialogue; a potential for minds to meet in the middle.

Together we advocate for communication through an antiquated form called "the handwritten letter." Believers in writing as a powerful means of expression. A sheet that can touch the heart, move the soul, inspire an ideal. This is the simplicity of a letter, in spirit.

The art of letter-writing is the establishment of that connection between the writer and the reader. Like a conversation – if you imagine it rewound many times and documented – what a handwritten letter captures is the imperfection and humanity of our inner voice and its power to connect.

Such was the strength of an open letter written by hand in 1963 from the discomfort of a jail cell in Birmingham, Alabama. There, Dr. Martin Luther King, Jr. penned his famous words that marked history forever: "Injustice anywhere is a threat to justice everywhere." In that long letter detailing oppression, Dr. Martin Luther King bled dry the shame of humanity. It was a handwritten letter: raw, real, relevant.

With the passage of decades, through re-reading and analysis, such handwritten letters surpass the confines of the period in which they are written. They become the testimony of vital signs, cherished by subsequent generations. Letters – to and from – document over time our social history.

In this flow of ideas, the private becomes public. Your faces now gain definition. My letter to you has opened a door. The seal of an invisible envelope is broken. The response is yours to craft.

March 22, 2015

Remarks by Judith Ravin at Minerva
"Handwritten with Love – The Art of Letter Writing"
House 4-A, Street 55, F-7/4, Islamabad

AFTERWARD

A N UNRAVELED THREAD JOINS THE END TO THE beginning in a circle moving counterclockwise. In that beginning, from a low-rise platform on a grassy stretch in Islamabad, I first launch an invitation to share the possibilities of dialogue and mutual exploration. I am reading a letter into a microphone, addressing a tight-knit crowd of largely unfamiliar faces.

An incoming response to my letter opens a door, taking the conversation in a direction no one could have predicted. How or when the thread connects door jams to entryways and departure lounges to moments of reckoning is esoterica outside the grasp of mere mortals. At some point a joint commitment becomes a weave of parallels finding natural points of connection between two disparate lives, past and present.

In essence, every letter harbors the potential for an opening, just as every closure sparks the search for alternative access. This counterpoint of two letters is the tale of many intersections.

A most intimate letter, meant for the eyes of a new bride only, meets the eyes of hundreds of thousands through its eventual publication, though I hear it read aloud for the first time from my place on the perimeter of a patch of lawn in Islamabad. It is among 180 such letters penned by its author to reaffirm love and to create an imaginary space of warmth that may ward off the effects of extended isolation.

By contrast, my public letter has no addressee. It advocates for validity in the first-person, and reclaims the raw simplicity of pen and paper when we are stripped of all else to restore dignity of purpose in a society that may intentionally choose to miss the point.

Timeless are letters to a beloved from Siachin. Timeless are letters to the world from jail. Timeless is my invitation to engage. The defiance of transcending limitations born from without is of greater consequence than sequence or its logic. Our two letters, this book, our push against closed doors, and a wish for new beginnings are a celebration of that freedom born from within.

ABOUT THE AUTHORS

JUDITH RAVIN

On assignment in Islamabad for the U.S. Department of State as Deputy Cultural Affairs Officer and later country Cultural Affairs Officer (2013-2015), Judith Ravin began her diplomatic career in 2003, after many years living and working abroad as an editor, translator, and journalist. In addition to Pakistan, she has worked in Mexico, Cameroon, Sudan, Dominican Republic, and the Office of the Haiti Special Coordinator in Washington, DC. For her next assignment, she will be based in Peru. Prior to becoming a Foreign Service Officer for the Department of State, she lived in Tokyo, where she was a Spanish-English translator for the Embassy of Peru, freelance editor for Kodansha International, and news rewriter for Fuji TV. Between extended stays in Tokyo and Buenos Aires, Ravin worked for the Ouagadougou-based *Journal du Jeudi* as a journalist and for the Pan-African Film and Television Festival of Ouagadougou (FESPACO) as a translator and editor. She is author of *Ballet in the Cane Fields* (bilingual edition, 2014), editorial-production team leader of *Traditional Tuti* (Khartoum, 2010), on-site researcher-writer for the Mali chapter of *The Rough Guide to West Africa* (special 2000 edition), and editor of travel guides *La Guía Pirelli Argentina 1995* and *La Guía Pirelli Uruguay* (1st edition, 1996). Ravin received a Master of Arts degree in Romance Languages and Literatures from Harvard University and a Bachelor of Arts in Spanish from Brandeis University. She also did undergraduate work in language, literature, and history at universities in France and Spain.

MUHAMMAD HASSAN MIRAJ

Muhammad Hassan Miraj is a creative writer, published author, and communication practitioner, yet remains at heart a storyteller. His 15-year career in the Pakistan Army took him across the country, enabling him to connect with ethnic and linguistic subcultures as well as the country's rich heritage of diverse lands and people. During his service for the Pakistan federal government, he also had the opportunity to visit Europe and to participate in an eight-month international visitor military exchange program in the United States (2009). Besides writing for the widely read English-language Pakistani daily *Dawn* since 2012, Miraj has also scripted short films and theatrical works. His first book, *Rail Ki Seeti* (Train Whistle, 2016), explores the impact of modernity and politics on rural landscape. Miraj is a documentary filmmaker, lyricist, and folklore specialist. His film

I Am Hazara was screened at the International Exile Film Festival and renown Museum of World Culture, in Sweden. Miraj pursued graduate studies in Media, Communication and Development at London School of Economics and Political Science, and is a graduate of National Defence University (Islamabad) and of Pakistan Military Academy (Kakul). He divides his time between the United Kingdom and Pakistan.

ACKNOWLEDGMENTS

JUDITH RAVIN

A list of all whose inspiration and sustenance nourished the seedling of an idea surpasses the limitations of this page. From my first "non-working day" of work in Pakistan, Dr. Nadeem Omar Tarar showed a keen interest in assuring my anthropological initiation. Likewise, Dr. Zeeshan ul-Hassan Usmani took joy in extending to me the full courtesies of cultural idiosyncrasy. Rooftop conversations with Hasan Ali, Sebastiano Giustiniani, Rakhshinda Perveen, Kahar Zalmay, and others under the glow of the Margalla Hills flooded my mind many times over with the excitement of possibility. At the U.S. Embassy in Islamabad – Syed Azfer Iqbal, Tanveer Hassan, Nadia Kamran, Shahid Waseem, Zarqa Yousaf, Sharif Sabir, Gulshan Batool, Saud Qureshi, Dilawar Khan, and others – as well as kindred spirits of public diplomacy at U.S. Consuls General in Lahore, Karachi, and Peshawar formed a welcoming gateway to all things Pakistani, presented in context. Endless cups of tea, a veiled excuse for the exchange of ideas on whatever, could be counted on in all variety of permutations with members of the contagiously dynamic Pakistan-U.S. Alumni Network (PUAN). These encounters in addition to geo-sessions with KMG and Musstanser Tinauli were ever enlightening. Periodic Sufi crosschecks courtesy of Sahibzada Asim Maharvi Chishti kept me on the spiritual up and up. To Muniba Mazari, I am grateful for her strength of spirit and for engendering on canvas a long line of stylized, pensive women equaled only by herself in beauty. Majid Saeed Khan and Morango Films taught me the impact of a tightly wound tale told within the constraints of extreme brevity. Soothing to the soul and my need for organized delirium were programs of cultural advocacy at Lok Virsa, including the annual folk festival, a gathering of artists and artisans from all corners of Pakistan. From kaleidoscopic jingle trucks I drew my daily breath, only to exhale in the timelessness of Qawwali. Through these art forms, I was able to embrace so much else. For frank humor and majestic melodies, I am graced by the friendship of Mekaal Hasan. While Raza Ali, overly wise for his years, imparted lessons on the charm of everyday objects. For holding myself and thousands of others spellbound at Music Mela, all my praise to the team at Foundation for Arts, Culture & Education, assisted by American and Pakistani colleagues plus a multitude of can-do volunteers. To those beyond the border – Rajiv Sethi, Sarika Sethi, Mohammad Hasan of Jaipur – travels to your side of history matured my regional vision. With deference, I thank co-author Muhammad Hassan Miraj, who intuited a place for me in his orbital space. To his other half, Dr. Amarah Kiani, I am thankful for her indulgence, as urgencies of word and print interrupted the daily rhythm of their lives. To anyone who ever provided feedback on my musings, thank you for reaffirming someone out there was listening. And although the book is an entirely personal undertaking, permission granted by leadership within the Bureau of South and Central Asian Affairs at the U.S. Department of State had an enabling effect on the project coming into being.

MUHAMMAD HASSAN MIRAJ

For all those who helped shape who I am. Southeastern Train Services and Transport for London, which kept on shunting across my thinking lanes. Roger Grey and the whole staff of the International Students Division, Fort Sill, Oklahoma (USA), for their tolerance of my impertinent questioning all those months. Iftikhar Ahmed Choudhry, one of the finest men I have met in the profession of arms. His calm listening is the reason I went on to express myself, more and more, though I was only a captain back then while he was a general. Asim Saleem Bajwa, for the phenomenal creative independence he gave me during my stay at Inter Services Public Relations (ISPR). Sarwar Mushtaq, a man of many seasons, is the reason I set sail. Every time he repeated his adage, "argue for your limitations, and they are yours forever," it made sense. Noonaris, Abdul Latif, and Shamila, for being the teachers one could only wish. Musadiq Sanwal, my late friend and editor at Dawn.com. Liaqat Ali Malik, the first officer who insisted that I should write, regardless of my surroundings. Aftab Iqbal Raja, probably the first one to stand up to the Pakistan Air Force recruitment system and tell them that they needed to adjust the rules rather than reject people on the basis of height and weight standards. Khurram Hanif Awan and Asad Mansoor for pushing me to join ISPR and opening an altogether new chapter of my life. Ajmal Khan, the sole sane voice accessible in the wonderland of upper foyer during Staff Course days. My class of Media Communication and Development at London School of Economics, especially Ambika, Jean, Chhavi, Terry, and Jessica, who really really want to change the world; and Shakuntala Banaji, the Guru, who deals with the ideal-ists and the realists alike. Bijli Topkhana, my home, for almost 15 years and counting. "Heer," Punjabi folklore that can rightly be called a phenomenon beyond worldly dimensions of time and space. Judith Ravin, for her con-tinuous support during the manifestation of this dream of ours. And finally, Amarah Kiani. It takes uncondi-tional love to wade through these waters.

CPSIA information can be obtained
at www.ICGtesting.com
Printed in the USA
BVOW03s0402270917
495979BV00017B/88/P